THE
PLANT LOVER'S GUIDE
TO
HARDY GERANIUMS

THE **PLANT LOVER'S GUIDE** TO
HARDY GERANIUMS

ROBIN PARER

TIMBER PRESS
PORTLAND, OREGON

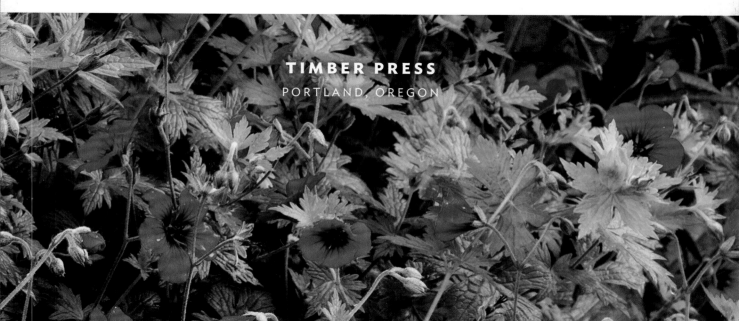

CONTENTS

41

140 Hardy Geraniums for the Garden

223

Growing and Propagating

WHY I LOVE HARDY GERANIUMS

Dennis Thompson, professor of horticulture and Seattle-based author, wrote:

> I want to live in a landscape, not the intensive-care ward of a plant hospital. Neither do I want my garden to be a prison where I must do bed checks nightly to be certain that someone isn't assaulting someone else. I assume plants are like children; there are going to be some squabbles, most of which they will work out themselves. If they can't work it out, eventually they will be separated. My garden has been fertilized with some exotic compost, but it is inhabited by hardy plants, and the genus *Geranium* offers some of the best.

In our overhybridized plant world, there is something calming and beautiful about wildflowers. While wandering around the countryside in spring, we come upon them as sheets of color carpeting meadows at low and high elevations, covering banks beside streams and roads, as starry flowers in forests, and even among the grasses on dunes at the seashore. We find ourselves wanting to capture these charming flowers and bring them closer to home.

Geranium nodosum 'Svelte Lilac' fills in a shady area under trees at Gossler Farms garden in Springfield, Oregon.

Some of the wildflowers we admire are hardy geraniums. Like pets, hardy geraniums adapt well to living in proximity to us. They settle down in gardens and provide seasonal bursts of flower color, as well as interesting leaves in shades of green but also silver, brown, gold, and maroon, with burnished cinnamon, red, orange, and bronze in fall. Despite their dramatic flair, they are not always the stars of the garden, but generally the supporting cast—tough, carefree, and easy to grow. Hardy geraniums last. It is not unusual for the same plant to be in a garden for decades, getting more and more beautiful as the years go on. And the flower colors yield such pleasure.

There are many blue, purple, violet, and lavender hardy geranium flowers. Blue is a favorite among gardeners, and it remains visible the longest during twilight. There are more than 50 different selections of hardy geraniums with blue, violet, purple, or lavender flowers. There are also innumerable shades of pink, plus white and magenta, which English plantsman A. E. Bowles called "that awful form of original sin." (His disparagement aside, magenta looks lovely with the yellow leaves of *Geranium* 'Ann Folkard'.) You can easily integrate these cool pink, white, and blue flowers into bedding schemes. There is only one red hardy geranium, and no yellow or orange flowers exist. There are very few double flowers, and the simplicity of the single flowers is unobtrusive and harmonizing.

As our climate becomes increasingly unpredictable, more and more we value plants that will survive drought, heavy rain, and intense heat and cold. Hardy geraniums, particularly those that come from challenging climates, are somewhat more adaptable to these conditions. Some gardeners have also tired of buying annuals, throwing them out at the end of the season, and bemoaning the amount of money spent. They are now turning to perennial plants.

Geranium 'Ann Folkard' makes an exuberant planting in the Thomas garden in Eugene, Oregon.

Most hardy geraniums are perennial. They are as easy as annuals to grow, if not easier, and they continue to perform through the seasons. And there is such variety. It is amazing that human-size *Geranium maderense*, from the island of Madeira, is related to the 4-inch (10 cm) alpine bun, *G. nanum*, from Morocco. The same is true for brilliant blue-flowered *G.* 'Rozanne' and the small brown-leafed *G. sessiliflorum* subsp. *novae-zelandiae* 'Nigricans' from New Zealand. It is easy for botanists to see the similarities, and not terribly difficult for gardeners to do the same. But more about that later. First we need to understand the term *hardy geranium*.

The word *geranium* has always had an identity crisis in the United States and Europe. It has been a case of botanists propose and gardeners oppose. If we wish to apportion blame, it begins with Carl Linnaeus, who in 1753 was the starting point for modern-day botanical nomenclature for seed plants. He did not distinguish between geraniums, which were (and still are) widespread in Europe, and the plants introduced into Europe from southern Africa, which we know now as pelargoniums. It wasn't until 1789 that Charles-Louis L'Heritier de Brutelle published the name Pelargonium. True geraniums, not the blanket term, are the subject of this book.

The confusion about the name persists 226 years later. And, moreover, are geraniums *cranesbills*, *hardy geraniums*, or, more ominously, *the other geraniums*? If only we could agree on a common name. Gardeners co-opted *geranium* for pelargoniums hundreds of years ago. Those who have inherited this tradition are unlikely to change, but gardeners must be able to distinguish true geraniums from pelargoniums.

Hardy geraniums are mostly herbaceous perennials. Most have perennial crowns and roots, and annual leaves and flowering stems. A few are woody subshrubs, and some are annuals. All the flowers have five equal-size petals and ten fertile (pollen-producing) stamens. You can find them in every country of the world except Antarctica. For those who don't like to delve into botany, there is practical benefit of growing hardy geraniums instead of pelargoniums: Within certain temperature boundaries, you can plant them in the garden and do not have to bring them inside and protect them during the winter.

Pelargoniums are mostly woody subshrubs. They maintain their woody structure throughout the growing season, and they do not disappear in the winter, unless killed off by cold and rain. They have flowers with five unequal-size petals, the two posterior usually larger than the three anterior. If the plant has a double flower, it is likely a pelargonium. Pelargonium flowers have 7 out of 10 fertile stamens, and a nectar tube that is fused to the outside of the pedicel and can be seen as a small bump. These plants mainly

Geranium palustre in a damp spot in a perennial border in Kentfield, California.

come from southern Africa and Australasia, which were joined as Gondwanaland, an ancient supercontinent, millions of years ago.

Hardy geranium seems like a reasonable compromise for a name. Pelargoniums are not usually winter hardy, as they come from mainly mild winter areas. The term *cranesbill*, used widely in Europe, has never been particularly popular on this side of the Atlantic, even though it is the English translation of the Greek *geranion*, which means crane. Geraniums got this name because of the structure of their seeds. The carpels containing the seeds resemble the head of the crane, and the bill or beak is the rostrum, the structure to which the awns, or tails, are attached. *Pelargonium* is derived from the Greek word for stork, and *erodium* for the Greek word for heron.

This book offers a fresh look at hardy geraniums. These plants have so much to recommend them, and are ideal for busy gardeners who long for beautiful flowers but do not want to hover over them worrying about complicated care regimes. Once established, hardy geraniums will do their own thing, and in our increasingly regimented, urbanized world, they provide a welcome touch of nature in our lives.

Lavender-blue flowered *Geranium* 'Nimbus' in a California mixed perennial garden.

DESIGNING WITH HARDY GERANIUMS

All gardeners, if they garden long enough, need plants that grow in shady places, cover bare patches in sun, and fill unsightly holes in planting schemes. Hardy geraniums can smother weeds, occupy awkward areas where other plants do not flourish, and provide seasonal flowers.

Ground Covers

Among hardy geraniums, the best ground covers are *Geranium macrorrhizum* and *G. ×cantabrigiense*. *Geranium macrorrhizum* is taller and has aromatic leaves, and it spreads by underground rhizomatous roots. *Geranium ×cantabrigiense*, a hybrid of *G. macrorrhizum* and *G. dalmaticum*, fulfills the same function, but is shorter and less aromatic. Both can cover large stretches in the garden, particularly in difficult spaces, such as the ground beneath and around shrubs and trees, in places that are full of competing roots, and in areas where a restful carpet of a single genus adds to a planting scheme. These plants come from the eastern end of the Mediterranean, so once established they are adapted

Both *Geranium ×cantabrigiense* 'Westray' and *G. ×oxonianum* 'Southcombe Star' make perfect ground covers for shady areas at the base of pines in the Reiners garden in Sacramento, California.

Geranium ×oxonianum 'Wargrave Pink' is a workhorse for light shade to morning sun areas.

to summer drought. Pests and diseases don't seem to bother them, and they require only good drainage. Flowers range in color from magenta to pink to white. Although they are not large, the flowers of *G. ×cantabrigiense* can be very attractive.

A third ground cover is *Geranium dalmaticum*. It is the smallest and covers less ground, but it achieves the same function as the other two. The plant spreads through the ground and chokes out weeds. All three geraniums tolerate morning sun and afternoon shade or light shade, and they are cold tolerant to USDA Zone 3.

Geranium endressii and *G. ×oxonianum* form clumps, and when planted close together can give the impression of a large, loose ground cover. Their mounding and spreading habits also prevent weeds. They remain in flower from early spring to mid-summer, when they start to look untidy and can be cut back to the crown, after which they will grow new leaves and flowers. They tolerate morning sun and afternoon shade and do well in areas where there is light or dappled shade. A possible downside is that *G. ×oxonianum* seeds wildly, so areas around the clumps may also fill with seedlings. These are not difficult to pull out, but you can lessen seed production by lightly cutting back in spring after the heavy flowering. The latter two geraniums also have a limited palette of white and pink, but *G. ×oxonianum* has very large range of quite dark to very pale pink flowers.

Some old cultivars are very well known. *Geranium ×oxonianum* 'Wargrave Pink' and *G. ×oxonianum* 'A. T. Johnson' are widely grown as ground covers and are well established in the nursery trade, as is *G. ×oxonianum* 'Claridge Druce'. *Geranium ×oxonianum* 'Katherine Adele' is a more recent addition, and has particularly desirable brown blotched leaves. There are also all kinds of color gradients of pink, so you can find just the right accent for a particular place.

Shade Lovers

Shade is one of the most challenging areas in the garden, especially because shady conditions can vary so widely. There is no substitute for observing your space during each of the four seasons. Light changes according to the path of the sun, so a garden that has light in spring may be in deep shade by fall. It is also important to consider the quality of shade. For example, does a particular area get no sun at all during the day, dappled shade, or shade only in the morning or afternoon? How long does the sunlight last? Each of these conditions can influence your decisions of what to plant where, but you have a large palette from which to choose: the different cultivated forms of *Geranium nodosum*, *G. cataractarum*, *G. palmatum*, *G. maderense*, and a wide selection of *G. phaeum* in various colors. *Geranium versicolor* has white flowers with an intricate pattern of purple veins. It seeds exuberantly but is a charming addition to a woodland garden.

Heavy shade is a challenge, and no hardy geranium looks its best in these conditions. But if you have reflected light off a patio or a wall, capture some of it to adjust conditions. You can do this by using light-colored paint or a large mirror, or by judiciously pruning nearby shrubs and trees. In an area that gets light only in spring and summer, the plant will become dormant in winter. When the light returns in spring, it is ready to start growing again.

Many shade geraniums do well in hot summer gardens with dry shade and cool, wet winters. Dry shade works, but you must water the plants to establish and grow through an entire season to develop sufficient roots to withstand a succeeding season with little or intermittent water.

The blue-and-white *Geranium* 'Rozanne', shown here in the Thomas garden, is one of the most popular and versatile geraniums ever produced.

Lovely *Geranium phaeum* 'Raven' at peak bloom in spring.

Beds and Borders

Many geraniums make large mounds or upright vase-shaped clumps that are perfect for beds and borders, such as *Geranium* 'Rozanne' or *G.* 'Orion'. Most tall-growing hardy geraniums (like *G.* ×*oxonianum* or *G.* 'Spinners') have a tendency to flop over, particularly in the first couple of years after planting, leaving a ruff of flowers around the edges with a mound of leaves in the center. You can correct this by pushing a horticultural corset of twigs into the ground around the plant to support the flowering stems so they grow upward instead of outward. As the clumps of growing points increase in size and width with age, this lax habit will wane. Another way to manage them is to plant other upright perennials close by so the flowering stems can lean against or grow through them.

The biggest obstacle to cultivating geraniums successfully is determining where to plant them and what type of soil they need. Once they are established, which generally

Geranium psilostemon 'Bressingham Flair' in the Ganzel garden in Cottage Grove, Oregon.

Geranium subcaulescens in the Parnell garden of El Dorado Hills, California.

takes a full growing season, hardy geraniums are mostly drought tolerant, depending on the quality of the soil, and require only moderate amounts of water. Mulching also helps to conserve water.

Although many hardy geraniums grow quickly, given good soil and moderate water, clump sizes—the number of growing points that form an individual clump—can be slow to develop, and often take up to three years to reach a good size. While you are waiting, you can fill space around them with other short-lived perennials or annuals.

Plant sizes vary considerably depending on soil quality, soil moisture, and summer temperatures. Many hardy geraniums are cold tolerant to at least 0°F (–18°C), and you can extend their tolerance by mulching or providing another kind of winter cover. The University of Chicago Botanic Garden has developed a chart recording the performance of 180 hardy geraniums in cold winter and humid summer conditions. However, if you are uncertain about a plant's performance under varied conditions, do a trial growth for at least one year in your garden before embarking on a large planting.

For color in a late-summer border, try *Geranium soboliferum* or its 'Butterfly Kisses' and 'Starman'. The species has dark red-pink petals with visible hairs on the upper petal surface. 'Butterfly Kisses' is a larger, sprawling plant. It has deep pink flowers with an intricate network of purple veins and some deeper shading of pink underneath them. 'Starman' has a compact habit and upright flowering stems. Its dark red-pink flowers have purple veins and long deep red-purple blotches on each petal.

Rock Gardens and Containers

Tidy, compact hardy geraniums are easy to grow in proper conditions. They often come from mountainous regions and some require alkaline soil. You can amend your soil, if necessary, by adding oyster grit, concrete chips, or careful doses of lime. You might like to try the *Geranium* Cinereum Group and its various named forms, or *G. farreri*. It is important to grow *G. argenteum* in a rock garden, as it seems to need absolutely perfect drainage. Some of the alpine geraniums have long root systems and do much better in soil that is porous or rocky. In hot summer gardens, it is still possible to grow these plants, but some light shade and even some misting during the day may be necessary to keep them alive.

The problem with growing rock garden plants in traditional garden beds is that the soil is often too heavy, the drainage is not sharp, and they can receive too much water, particularly from general irrigation systems. Plants growing on either side can also overwhelm hardy geraniums. In this situation, a rock garden, trough, or container is preferable. You will have more control over soil conditions and will be better equipped to provide excellent drainage.

Rock gardens and traditional troughs are very useful, and if you have them in your garden you should take advantage of them to grow these plants, but drainage pipes, chimney pots, or tall terra-cotta containers are acceptable substitutes. In hot summer gardens it may be necessary to use double pots or thick walled containers for some sensitive plants, such as *Geranium argenteum*, which likes to have cool roots.

Geranium regelii resembles a diminutive form of *G. pratense*. Although it produces only a few flowers in midsummer, it has value because of its small size. Its roots appear to grow to considerable depths, so rocky, gravelly, sharp drainage is a must when growing this alpine species.

Early summer-flowering *Geranium pratense* 'Wisley Blue' in a perennial border at the Ganzel garden in Oregon.

Favorite Geraniums from Garden Professionals

One of the best ways to learn how to incorporate hardy geraniums into a garden is to study how expert gardeners use them in various settings. The specialists profiled here represent a wide range of climates and growing conditions.

- Mary Ann Brady has a nursery and design business in southeastern Massachusetts (Zone 6b) and specializes in hardy geraniums.
- Panayoti Kelaidis gardens in Denver (Zone 5b) and is an adventurous promoter of interesting garden plants.
- Glenn Withey and Charles Price have a landscape design business in Seattle (Zone 8b), and have had considerable experience in planting hardy geraniums and judging their usefulness in their designs.
- Connie Umberger lives and gardens in challenging conditions on the island of Nantucket (Zone 7b) off the coast of Massachusetts, and has been a devotee of hardy geraniums for many years.
- Judy Horton designs gardens in the Los Angeles area (Zone 10) and is responding in her designs to the years-long drought in southern California.
- Craig Bergmann Landscape Design is a full-service landscape architectural and design firm in Lake Forest, Illinois (Zone 5b).
- Elise Zylstra is manager of Sandy's Plants, a nursery in central Virginia (Zone 7a) with a large list of hardy geraniums.

Mary Ann Brady operates a small specialty nursery in New England devoted to unusual plants. She is also a garden designer and uses hardy geraniums in many of her creations. "I never think formal when talking about geraniums," she notes. Instead, she goes for "natural looking, especially because I cut a lot of them back when bloom is over to let them refresh themselves." The harsh winters so typical of the region require that all pots be brought indoors, so Mary Ann rarely uses geraniums in containers.

For a sunny garden, Mary Ann's favorite is *Geranium* 'Rozanne' because it provides so much color for the entire summer. Other showstoppers are *G. sanguineum* 'Elke', *G.* 'Pink Penny', and *G.* 'Sweet Heidy', which has a large pale center and rainbow of outer rings that change from pink to purple

Mary Ann Brady

CRANESBILL NURSERY
Swansea, Massachusetts
Zone 6b

FAVORITES FOR SUN

- G. (Cinereum Group) 'Ballerina'
- G. *maculatum* 'Album'
- G. 'Orion'
- G. ×*oxonianum* 'Claridge Druce'
- G. 'Pink Penny'
- G. *pratense* 'Mrs. Kendall Clark'
- G. *pratense* 'Striatum'
- G. 'Rozanne'
- G. *sanguineum* 'Elke'
- G. 'Sweet Heidy'

FAVORITES FOR SHADE

- G. ×*cantabrigiense* 'Biokovo'
- G. ×*cantabrigiense* 'St. Ola'
- G. *macrorrhizum* 'Spessart'
- G. *maculatum* 'Espresso'
- G. *phaeum* 'Calligrapher'
- G. *phaeum* 'Chocolate Chip'
- G. *phaeum* 'Lily Lovell'
- G. *phaeum* 'Samobor'
- G. *renardii*
- G. 'Stephanie'
- G. *wlassovianum*

as the flowers age. Mary Ann sees the role of most geraniums as supporting because of bloom times.

In shady gardens, Mary Ann favors *Geranium* 'Stephanie', with very beautiful foliage and great flowers, and *G. macrorrhizum* 'Spessart', a warhorse ground cover whose leaves have a wonderful scent. *Geranium ×cantabrigiense* 'Biokovo' and *G. ×cantabrigiense* 'St. Ola' are invaluable ground covers. For good foliage in shady situations, Mary Ann recommends *G. renardii*, *G. phaeum* 'Calligrapher', and *G. phaeum* 'Samobor'.

Two good plants for drought tolerance are *Geranium sanguineum* and *G. cinereum*. Mary Ann does not like some of the new hybrids, which are bred too tightly and do not survive in gardens without cosseting.

Among the companion plants that Mary Ann uses in her designs, she loves *Kirengeshoma palmata* for fall color and as a backdrop. Her favorite companion plant for shade is *Brunnera* 'Jack Frost'. Other options are rodgersia, ligularia, pulmonaria, astrantia, cimicifuga, dicentra, epimedium, heuchera, anenome, and polygonatum. For sunny spots, her favorite companion is *Amsonia hubrectii*, which has fabulous fall color. Two close relatives that also work well are *A. tabernaemontana* and *A. orientalis*. Mary Ann also suggests sedum, crocosmia, asclepia, monarda, perovskia, papaver, potentilla, and rudbeckia.

Panayoti Kelaidis is senior curator and director of outreach at the Denver Botanic Gardens. He also writes about plants and has been on many plant expeditions to all parts of the world. He has a fascinating rock garden of his own, and his favorite hardy geraniums for rock gardens are *Geranium argenteum*, *G.* (Cinereum Group) 'Ballerina', *G. sanguineum* var. *striatum*, *G. orientaltibeticum*, *G. subcaulescens*, *G. mieboldii*, *G. nanum*, *G. pyrenaicum* 'Bill Wallis', and *G. sessiliflorum* subsp. *novaezelandiae* 'Nigricans'.

The climate in Denver is dramatic, characterized by highly cold winters and extremely hot summers. Many plants that are not hardy in wetter climates may survive here because of a long, dry hardening-off period in fall. Denver is part of the Colorado Front Range, a semi-arid continental region otherwise known as steppe. Few geraniums grow naturally on the short grass prairie, which is too sunny and dry for them to persist, but geraniums quickly appear if you gain a bit of altitude among the pines in sparse grasses. With even occasional irrigation, a wide spectrum of geraniums quickly adapts to garden settings.

Panayoti likens the wonderful blues and lavenders of hardy geraniums to the violin section of an orchestra.

Panayoti Kelaidis

DENVER BOTANIC GARDENS
Denver
Zone 5b

FAVORITES FOR SUN

G. caespitosum
G. magniflorum
G. pratense 'Midnight Reiter'
G. 'Rozanne'
G. sanguineum

FAVORITES FOR SHADE

G. 'Ann Folkard'
G. ×cantabrigiense
G. dalmaticum
G. macrorrhizum
G. maculatum
G. renardii
G. sanguineum

FAVORITES FOR ROCK GARDENS

G. argenteum
G. (Cinereum Group) 'Ballerina'
G. mieboldii
G. nanum
G. orientaltibeticum
G. pyrenaicum 'Bill Wallis'
G. sanguineum var. striatum
G. sessiliflorum subsp. novaezelandiae 'Nigricans'

They are essential in the garden because of their durability, long season of beauty, and contrast to other garden plants. Some, like *Geranium psilostemon*, have striking flowers that provide a focal point of interest. Most of the soft blue flowered sorts provide the perfect foils for brighter yellow, orange, or red companions. Panayoti asserts that although most geraniums have a long blooming season (in the case of *G.* 'Rozanne', almost too long), their distinctive and always attractive masses of foliage earn them star billing. In fact, so many geraniums have gorgeous fall color that he values them almost as much for their autumnal fire as for the cool flowers of spring and summer.

Obviously, geraniums are essential for the classic English perennial border based on lavender and pastel pinks and blues, but most geraniums also provide a wonderful underplanting and contrast for many bulbs, including daffodils in spring, foxtail lilies of summer, and colchicums in autumn. Many of these bulbs will grow when planted right in among the geraniums. Because geraniums have such distinctive scalloped or divided but rounded leaves of moderate size, they practically demand to be combined with the linear and

Glenn Withey and Charles Price

WITHEY PRICE LANDSCAPE AND DESIGN
Seattle
Zone 8b

FAVORITES FOR SUN

G. 'Ann Folkard'
G. 'Blue Sunrise'
G. ×*cantabrigiense*
   'Biokovo'
G. (Cinereum Group)
   'Ballerina'
G. 'Mavis Simpson'
G. 'Orion'
G. 'Rozanne'
G. 'Sue Crûg'
G. 'Tiny Monster'

FAVORITES FOR SHADE

G. *macrorrhizum* 'Album'
G. *macrorrhizum*
   'Cham Ce'
G. *macrorrhizum* 'Czakor'
G. *macrorrhizum*
   'White-Ness'
G. *maculatum* 'Elizabeth
   Ann'
G. *phaeum* 'Advendo'
G. *phaeum* var. *lividum*
G. *phaeum* var. *lividum*
   'Majus'
G. *phaeum* var. *lividum*
   'Walküre'
G. *phaeum* 'Tricia'

Geranium 'Patricia' is a wonderful long-flowering summer addition to the O'Byrne garden in Eugene, Oregon.

Flowering *Geranium macrorrhizum* as a ground cover on a hillside in a Pennsylvania garden

sword-shaped leaves of daylilies or the mounding form of hostas. They are so versatile and adaptable, there is a geranium for almost any other garden plant or form. The possibilities are endless.

Traditionally, Rocky Mountain gardeners have not grown many perennials in containers, but this is changing. Most European geraniums have proved to be quite hardy and will overwinter in larger containers, but you can transfer some that are touch and go, like *Geranium* 'Rozanne', from a container to the soil in late summer.

According to Panayoti, alpine geraniums have a special niche growing in trough gardens. You can tuck in many of the smaller species among rocks. Some, like *Geranium dalmaticum*, will spill over the edge of the trough, and their brilliant orange fall foliage is almost as gorgeous as the bright pink flowers in early summer.

Ground-covering geraniums make neat mats of clean foliage. You can use them in formal edgings and mass plantings, but they look just as fetching planted informally in clumps in the xeriscape or naturalistic wild gardens. You can less easily incorporate the larger, coarser forms of *Geranium pratense*, for example, in formal plantings. Panayoti values *G. macrorrhizum* and *G. ×cantabrigiense* for their tolerance of deep shade; once established, they also are extremely drought tolerant. Because they are so easily managed in the shade, he recommends them to all gardeners as the ideal ground cover under trees and shrubs.

Glenn Withey and Charles Price specialize in the design, installation, and maintenance of residential and city gardens on both coasts. They have worked with clients to develop gardens with year-round interest or for display during a specific season. They are masters of color and texture, and they have designed some of the most beautiful and exciting gardens in North America.

Glenn and Charles use geraniums for floral color and outstanding foliage. Among their favorites for sun are *Geranium* 'Rozanne', *G.* 'Ann Folkard', *G.* 'Mavis Simpson', and *G.* 'Orion'. For shade, they are partial to various forms of *G. phaeum*, including 'Tricia', 'Advendo', var. *lividum*, and its cultivars 'Walküre' and 'Majus'. When growing sun-demanding plants in Seattle's wet weather, give them adequate space; crowding will cause them to get weak and floppy.

Well-grown massive plants like *Geranium* 'Ann Folkard', *G. psilostemon*, *G. maderense*, and *G. palmatum* are stars in the garden. Masses of color from *G. himalayense*, *G.* ×*magnificum*, *G. ibericum*, and *G. sanguineum* can reach stellar performances, but they are lower than most shrubs and many other herbaceous plants, and are considered supporting cast.

Good companion plants include spring and early summer alliums, early narcissus species and hybrids (so their foliage has a chance before the geraniums completely shade them out), tulips (mostly as annuals), galanthus in damper or shady areas, taller-growing lilies, roses, tree peonies, upright ferns in shaded areas, upright-foliaged and taller-blooming grasses, *Iris siberica*, *I. ensata*, and *I.* ×*pseudata*. Early flowering rock garden peonies are excellent with low sun-loving geraniums.

The lavish late spring bloom of *Geranium pratense* 'Victor Reiter' with *G.* 'Nimbus' in an Oregon garden.

For container planting, Glenn and Charles suggest *Geranium phaeum* for large shade pots. For edging sunny pots, they recommend scramblers like *G. ×riversleaianum* 'Russell Prichard' and *G.* 'Mavis Simpson'.

Because of their wide variety of overall forms, geraniums are amenable to any style of garden. For Japanese gardens, consider *Geranium dalmaticum* or *G. sessiliflorum* hybrids in open-stone arrangement areas, or a few plants of *G. phaeum* emerging from the moss in an open place in a wooded stroll garden. Geraniums are suitable for wild, naturalistic, and cottage styles, as well as bedding in formal rose gardens and hedged parterres. The only cautionary note is to beware of all forms of *G. ×oxonianum* and *G. pratense*, which can seed violently in the Seattle area.

Connie Umberger gardens on Nantucket Island in a climate of hard winters and hot, muggy summers. She is a recipient of the Massachusetts Horticultural Society gold medal and a founder of the Nantucket Garden Festival. She claims to be a "totally amateurish trial and error gardener with a taste for avoidance of rules, considerable chaos, and inability to control my appetite for more and more plants, but somehow managing nevertheless to create quite personal gardens that people seem to like, although at the same time probably decimating my children's inheritance."

Nantucket is situated in the Gulf Stream, and thus warmer than mainland Massachusetts, and does not normally have snow cover for insulation. Winters most commonly consist of repeated freezes and thaws, which are not ideal for perennial plants regardless of their listed degree of hardiness. The island's soil is nothing but sand. Sun, humidity, and wind abound. In summer, there is little rain.

Connie likes geraniums because "they are just plain fun." In the right situation, they provide a cheerful, vivacious, yet somehow unassuming nonchalance that enlivens more formal, stiffer neighbors. They are wonderful for their distinctive foliage alone, especially the bronze and brown, which contrasts strikingly with other plants. Bloom at its best is blazing, especially for the blue-flowering specimens.

When in bloom geraniums speak volumes, and can be quite astonishing if nothing else is flowering at the same time. Otherwise their role is that of a wonderful supporting cast that provides lively contrast as well as complement. Connie declares, "I know of no other plant that so perfectly enhances whatever it's next to; in this way it's very much like lady's mantle—it makes everything else look better." In her gardens, geraniums are indispensable.

Connie Umberger

Nantucket Island, Massachusetts
Zone 7b

FAVORITES FOR SUN

G. ×magnificum
G. 'Nimbus'
G. 'Orion'
G. ×oxonianum 'Claridge Druce'
G. ×oxonianum 'Wageningen'
G. ×oxonianum 'Wargrave Pink'
G. 'Philippe Vapelle'
G. ×riversleaianum 'Russell Prichard'
G. 'Rozanne'
G. 'Sandrine'

FAVORITES FOR SHADE

G. maculatum 'Elizabeth Ann'
G. maculatum 'Espresso'
G. renardii
Almost all forms of G. phaeum, especially 'Lily Lovell'

Geranium sanguineum var. *striatum* and *G. ×cantabrigiense* 'Biokovo' form companion ground covers in the Thomas garden.

According to Connie, most plants look good with geraniums, especially grasses like the yellow and brown carexes and hakonechloas. Geraniums are good companions for roses, bergenias, hostas, iris, and euphorbias, as well as with each other when arranged in complementary (as opposed to similar) bloom colors. They do well under smallish shrubs, where the clamberers do their thing among the low branches of the shrubs, thus adding interest.

Many of the geraniums listed for rock gardens and containers are not hardy enough for siting outdoors on Nantucket, but Connie plants them in clay pots that look great (and interesting) collected together on the terrace from late spring to late fall, and then moves them into the greenhouse for the winter, where they do amazingly well at around 50°F (10°C), or more on sunny days. Her collection includes *Geranium ×antipodeum* 'Stanhoe', *G. ×antipodeum* 'Chocolate Candy', *G.* 'Dusky Crûg', *G. sessiliflorum* 'Coffee 'n Cream', *G.* (Cinereum Group) 'Alice', and *G.* (Cinereum Group) 'Carol', all of which are highly desirable.

Geraniums are not limited to any particular garden style. Connie uses them in both formal and naturalistic gardens; scattered in a very casual narrow border among low grasses and odds and ends along a long boundary fence; in cracks between stones in a somewhat formal terrace and in gravel

Judy Horton

JUDY M. HORTON GARDEN DESIGN
Los Angeles
Zone 10

FAVORITES FOR SUN

G. 'Brookside'
G. incanum
G. maderense
G. 'Rozanne'
G. sanguineum

FAVORITES FOR SHADE

G. ×cantabrigiense 'Biokovo'
G. ×oxonianum 'Katherine Adele'

An unusual container planting of *Geranium sanguineum* 'Nyewood' among perennial herbs in the Reiners garden.

among epimediums, grasses, and hostas in mostly shade; and as color to fill in the curves of a meandering boxwood snake in full sun on either side of a long rill. There is sure to be at least one geranium that is perfect for whatever vagary might present itself in your space.

Judy Horton thinks of herself as a plantswoman and a maker of places. She has been a garden designer in southern California for more than 20 years. Mostly self-taught, she has been widely published in lifestyle magazines and has written three books about her gardens.

At one time Judy had a mixed border of roses, perennials, flowering and fruiting shrubs, and many geraniums. Over time she has whittled down the geraniums to a few select plants. Today her space and most of her clients' gardens are filled with Mediterranean-climate plants that need little water in summer. Her garden style is naturalistic.

Foliage is the main reason Judy uses geraniums. Her favorite ground covers in light shade or under deciduous trees are *Geranium* ×*cantabrigiense* 'Biokovo' and *G.* ×*oxonianum* 'Katherine Adele' (albeit not together).

In sunny gardens that call for a diva, Judy turns to *Geranium maderense*. Elsewhere, she likes to grow *G.* 'Rozanne' and *G.* 'Brookside' on the north side of roses. *Geranium sanguineum*, another of her favorite sun-lovers, gives a great blast of color in a summer or fall border of purple and magenta salvias, clipped myrtle, and euphorbia.

Containers are not a big part of Judy's designs, but she has paired *Geranium* 'Ann Folkard' with an itea. The geranium was fantastic for the three years it lasted, climbing up into the twisty itea branches. The color combination was perfect in fall, when the itea leaves turned the color of wine. Seeing the geranium up high, almost at eye level, was a special treat. Unfortunately, the geranium succumbed to root competition from the itea.

If a plant cannot thrive for five years, Judy no longer uses it. Besides *Geranium* 'Ann Folkard', other has-beens on her list are *G.* ×*magnificum*, *G. phaeum*, *G.* 'Philippe Vapelle', and *G. renardii*.

Craig Bergmann Landscape Design (CBLD) is a full-service landscape architecture and design firm. The company has worked in the lower Great Lakes region for three decades and is known for its unique intertwining of design, horticulture, and architecture.

Craig Bergmann Landscape Design Team

Lake Forest, Illinois
Zone 5b

FAVORITES FOR SUN

- G. ×*cantabrigiense* 'Biokovo'
- G. ×*cantabrigiense* 'Karmina'
- G. ×*magnificum*
- G. 'Rozanne'
- G. *sanguineum*
- G. *sanguineum* 'Album'
- G. *sanguineum* 'Max Frei'

FAVORITES FOR SHADE

- G. ×*cantabrigiense* cultivars, especially 'Biokovo'
- G. *macrorrhizum* 'Album'
- G. *macrorrhizum* 'Bevan's Variety'
- G. *macrorrhizum* 'Ingwersen's Variety'
- G. *maculatum*
- G. *phaeum*

One of CBLD's favorite geraniums for sun is *Geranium* 'Rozanne'. This famous hybrid is best for overall floral effect because of its long bloom time. It has a vigorous, spreading habit, so it works well along the edges of walls and as a ground cover. Its foliage does not have a major decline after initial flowering, and this contributes to its overall good looks throughout the growing season. Some dead leafing and selective pruning will keep the plant looking better. *Geranium* 'Rozanne' may not play well with others because of its exuberant spreading, but for that very reason it makes a good ground cover for a full bed under formal trees.

Geranium sanguineum, another favorite for sunny sites, and *G. macrorrhizum*, a darling in shady spots, are stars in the garden when in flower, neutral when not, and stars again for fall foliage effect. Both are reliable performers. *Geranium macrrohizum* and cultivars have the added benefit of scented foliage. Like *G.* 'Rozanne', *G. sanguineum* makes a good ground cover for a full bed under formal trees.

Geranium phaeum is a little finicky to grow, as it must have ideal conditions and shade. Nonetheless, it is a unique little geranium for the ambitious gardener.

The CBLD team uses most geraniums in casual garden borders. The ground-covering types are nice companions with hedges in formal settings. *Geranium maculatum* is useful in the mixed border garden for spring. *Geranium ×cantabrigiense* 'Biokovo' and *G. macrorrhizum* 'Ingwersen's Variety' excel in naturalistic gardens.

Good companions for *Geranium ×magnificum* (and other earlier violet-blue cultivars) are peony, lady's mantle, and yellow loosestrife. Unfortunately, *G. ×magnificum* can be difficult to use because of foliage decline after flowering (although the spectacular flower display makes it worth planting). To remedy this, combine it with midsummer perennials, such as coneflowers, asters, and daisies, that will provide interest until the foliage recovers. Companions for *G. sanguineum* and cultivars include perennial allium, bearded iris, and perennial salvia. *Geranium* 'Perfect Storm' is suitable for container plantings.

Elise Zylstra is sales manager for Sandy's Plants, a Virginia nursery that specializes in supplying rare and unusual perennials to the east coast. Whether geraniums are grown in the region in sun or shade, the nursery recommends some protection from the hottest afternoon sun for all varieties.

For sun, *Geranium macrorrhizum* and its cultivars are particularly popular with landscapers in the area (one uses them almost exclusively). They make an excellent, super hardy ground cover. *Geranium* 'Rozanne' is always popular, and is still Sandy's favorite. *Geranium ×cantabrigiense* 'Biokovo' and *G. ×cantabrigiense* 'Karmina' are also used extensively, and after observing them in Sandy's gardens, Elise thinks they are superior performers to

Elise Zylstra

SANDY'S PLANTS
Mechanicsville, Virginia
Zone 7a

FAVORITES FOR SUN

G. ×cantabrigiense 'Biokovo'
G. ×cantabrigiense 'Cambridge'
G. ×cantabrigiense 'Karmina'
G. macrorrhizum
G. 'Rozanne'
G. 'Tiny Monster'

FAVORITES FOR SHADE

G. maculatum
G. maculatum 'Album'

A spreading group of *Geranium clarkei* 'Kashmir White' in a spring border at the Perryman Whitman garden in Oregon.

'Rozanne', although not as showy in bloom. They do not get the leggy, sprawling habit that afflicts 'Rozanne' if it is not cut back.

One of Sandy's landscapers uses lots of *Geranium* 'Tiny Monster' in sunny sites because it has a long bloom time and the flowers are a clean, rich magenta. *Geranium* 'Rozanne', *G.* ×*cantabrigiense* 'Biokovo', *G.* ×*cantabrigiense* 'Karmina', and *G.* ×*cantabrigiense* 'Cambridge' also perform in the sun. Likewise, *G. macrorrhizum* and cultivars do fairly well in this situation, but definitely appreciate a little more moisture.

Probably the best for full shade in Sandy's area is *Geranium maculatum*, a woodland native. It prefers moist soil and may become dormant in summer if it is too dry, but it is an amazing survivor even in arid situations. It will also do well in partial sun. There is a white version, *G. maculatum* 'Album'. Unfortunately, neither is commonly available and Sandy's has them only sporadically.

Experience at Sandy's has shown that *Geranium* ×*cantabrigiense* 'Biokovo', *G.* ×*cantabrigiense* 'Karmina', and *G.* ×*cantabrigiense* 'Cambridge' often look best in nursery pots, but for containers, *G. sanguineum* 'Max Frei' is one of the best because it is very compact. *Geranium* ×*cantabrigiense* 'Cambridge' is another compact cultivar that would work well in pots.

None of the geraniums are thought of as formal, although the tighter forms, such as *Geranium* ×*cantabrigiense* 'Biokovo', are suitable for formal situations. *Geranium* 'Rozanne' is definitely informal and makes a really good weaver between other perennials. *Geranium maculatum* and cultivars are probably the most naturalistic. The boldest are *G. macrorrhizum* and cultivars, with their big leaves and large growth habit. *Geranium sanguineum* var. *striatum* is one of the daintiest looking, with its delicate bloom color, small leaves, and low habit.

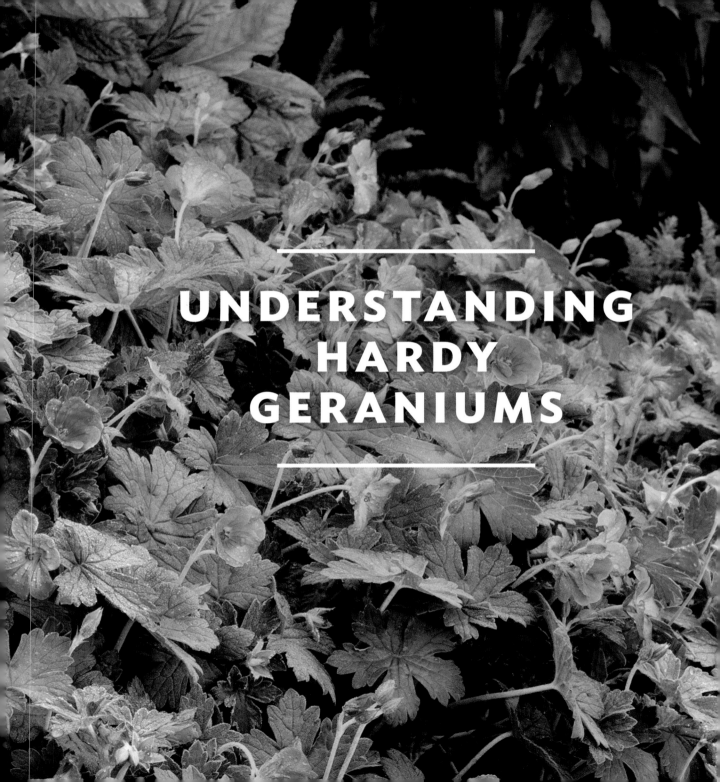

UNDERSTANDING HARDY GERANIUMS

Geranium pratense 'Galactic' at Gossler Farms garden.

In the 1980s, the United States experienced an upsurge of interest in perennial gardens, and hardy geraniums began to appear on the radar. Many gardeners and garden writers, perhaps looking for new and interesting trends, made obligatory visits to famous perennial gardens in Germany, the Netherlands, and the United Kingdom, and returned with tales of glorious vistas filled with hardy geraniums and grasses, evoking among serious gardeners plant envy and the desire for something new. Gradually hardy geraniums started appearing in gardens, nurseries, botanic gardens, and plant collections all over the country.

After the initial enthusiasm, which lasted for about three decades, there was some retrenchment. *The Plant Finder*, an annual compendium of plants available in the United Kingdom, continued to swell with more and more hardy geraniums, but in the United States gardeners took refuge in planting the old varieties, such as *Geranium ×oxonianum* 'Wargrave Pink' or *G. ×oxonianum* 'A. T. Johnson', which had been around for decades. Possibly these hardy geraniums were

reliably present in local nurseries in the spring. Some geraniums did, however, get everyone's attention. *Geranium* 'Rozanne' has sold more than 6 million plants and is one of the most widely planted of the hardy geraniums—so much so that there have been many efforts to duplicate its success.

Ground cover geraniums, which tolerate a wide range of climatic conditions, have never stopped being popular. But many hardy geraniums are a bit like seven-day wonders. They are initially subject to vigorous publicity campaigns, but after a couple of years they are difficult to find in nurseries or on lists, or they have disappeared. All gardeners can do is keep asking for favorites and apply pressure through retail nurseries and indirectly to their wholesalers to keep propagating.

There are about 420 species of hardy geraniums. They are found mainly in the cool, temperate areas of the world. You can find geraniums in countries from the United States, Mexico, and Central and South America to Europe, Asia, Africa, and many oceanic islands. They are most frequently plants of forests, meadows, and scrublands, although there are some high alpine species and some species that live in hot, arid areas. They generally range in height from 4 to 60 inches (10–150 cm), depending on the species. There is even a tree, or rather a large shrub, *Geranium arboreum*, from the island of Maui, which grows to about 12 feet (3.6 m). Most geraniums are herbaceous perennials. Some maintain their leaves in winter in mild climates, and some, like those from southern Africa, the islands in the Atlantic and from Hawaii, are evergreen. There are also a few garden-worthy annuals, but there is also an overabundance of annual and perennial weedy species that gardeners rightfully ignore.

Taxonomist Peter Yeo's monograph, *Hardy Geraniums*, contains the most useful and complete plant descriptions for botanists and enthusiastic gardeners looking to identify hardy geranium species. There are also many books, some unfortunately out of print, that describe different species and cultivars for the home gardener. The Internet is a source for information on hardy geraniums, but different sites provide wildly variable information on sizes, flower colors, and seasons of bloom. Be sure to consult two or three different sites for the same plant. The Plantsman's Preference website from the United Kingdom has careful, useful information and good photos, but be aware that culture can greatly change plant size, and English words for flower color are not standardized.

Leaves

Geraniums generally form basal rosettes of leaves from which elongating flowering stems will grow. Foliage is often present on the flowering stems, although these leaves may differ from the basal rosette leaves in size and number of lobes. Geranium leaves are often highly variable in size, ranging from 1/2 inch (1.3 cm) (*Geranium sessiliflorum* subsp. *novaezelandiae* 'Nigricans') to more than 15 inches (38 cm) (*G. maderense*), but many of the species have leaves that are 2 to 6 inches (5–15 cm). Most leaves have a roughly palmate shape. Some are entire and lightly scalloped, and some are deeply lobed and dissected. Many are toothed around the leaf margin. The leaves range in color from deep brown (*G.* 'Dusky Crûg') or light brown (*G. maculatum* 'Elizabeth Ann') through gray (*G. traversii* var. *elegans*), or gray-green (*G.* (Cinereum Group) 'Ballerina') to silver (*G. argenteum*) to bright glossy green (*G. ×cantabrigiense*) to medium green and hairy (*G. platyanthum*) to dark green (*G. sanguineum*). Some geraniums have light yellow-green markings on the leaves (*G. wallichianum* 'Buxton's Variety' and *G. orientaltibeticum*). Some have maroon internodal blotches on the leaves (*G. phaeum* 'Samobor', *G. ×monacense* 'Muldoon', *G. versicolor*). There is a very small number of variegated leaf geraniums. *Geranium phaeum* 'Variegatum' has cream-and-pink variegated new leaves, *G. phaeum* 'Taff's Jester' has cream splashes and stippling on the leaves, and *G. ×oxonianum* 'Margin of Error' has irregular cream edges. A few geraniums have bright yellow leaves when they first emerge from the ground in the spring (*G. phaeum* 'Mrs. Withey-Price', *G.* 'Sandrine', *G.* 'Blue Sunrise'), but most turn yellow-green by midsummer. The endless variety of leaves provides one of the strongest reasons why gardens might want to grow hardy geraniums.

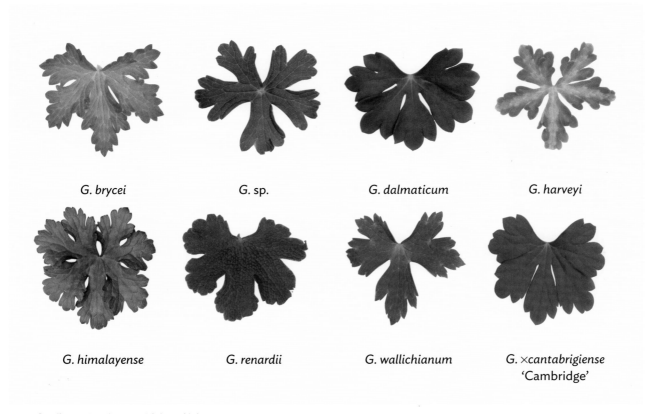

G. brycei	*G.* sp.	*G. dalmaticum*	*G. harveyi*
G. himalayense	*G. renardii*	*G. wallichianum*	*G. ×cantabrigiense* 'Cambridge'

Small geranium leaves with broad lobes.

G. phaeum 'Samobor'

G. 'Ann Folkard'

G. pratense
'Black Beauty'

G. 'Blue Sunrise'

G. 'Dusky Crûg'

G. phaeum
'Margaret Wilson'

G. 'Orkney Dawn'

G. maculatum
'Elizabeth Ann'

G. phaeum
'Springtime'

G. phaeum
'Variegatum'

G. sessiliflorum
subsp. novaezelandiae
'Nigricans'

G. thunbergii
'Jester's Jacket'

G. ×oxonianum
'Katherine Adele'

Colored geranium leaves.

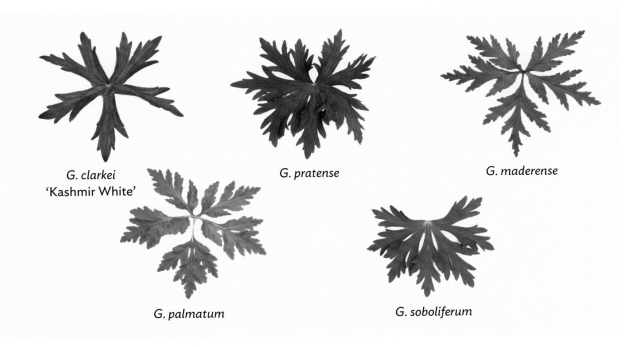

G. clarkei
'Kashmir White'

G. pratense

G. maderense

G. palmatum

G. soboliferum

Large geranium leaves with narrow lobes.

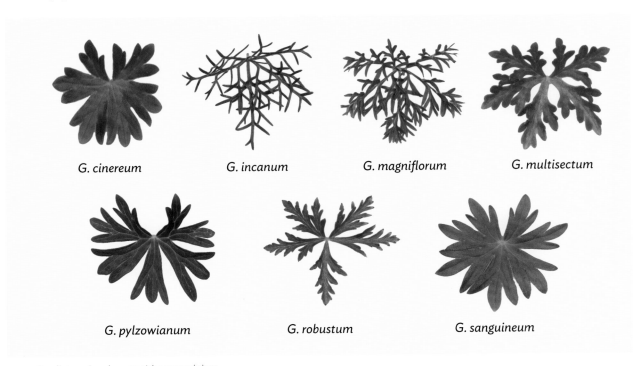

G. cinereum

G. incanum

G. magniflorum

G. multisectum

G. pylzowianum

G. robustum

G. sanguineum

Small geranium leaves with narrow lobes.

G. erianthum

G. ibericum

G. macrorrhizum

G. maculatum

G. viscosissimum

G. nodosum

G. phaeum

G. platypetalum

G. psilostemon

G. sylvaticum

G. wlassovianum

G. ×oxonianum
'Wargrave Pink'

Large geranium leaves with broad lobes.

Flowers

In many of the geranium species, flowering occurs in flushes. Geranium flowers are blue, lavender, purple, pink, white, and magenta, and many variations within those colors. Most flowers have veins in light, dark, or contrasting hues, and sometimes the veins coalesce at the base of the petals to form blotches, or there are splashes of deeper or contrasting color on the petals. The flower colors combine best with other flowers in the blue-red side of the color spectrum, particularly with blue, cream, and pink flowers of other perennials and shrubs. For some people, planting hardy geraniums with flowers of clear red poses a problem. But it is all a matter of taste. There are no yellow or orange geraniums and no clear reds, unless you include the cherry-colored geranium species (*Geranium* sp.) from New Mexico and Durango, Mexico.

Geranium flowers have five equal-size petals. The structure of the flower includes five sepals; ten fertile stamens in two whorls, or rings that open successively; and five carpels, the structures that contain the seeds. Noting the structure is the easiest way to distinguish geraniums from pelargoniums. The flowers of hardy geraniums are usually $\frac{1}{2}$ to $2\frac{1}{2}$ inches (1.25–6 cm) in diameter. Geraniums generally produce their flowers on ever-lengthening annual flowering stems during the growing season. Flowering stems may eventually become quite untidy, so cut them back at some point. The plant will usually, but not always, produce more flowering stems if the weather and season are conducive.

Fruit

All plants in Geraniaceae have a very characteristic fruit with a narrow beak-like structure rising up from a cluster of seeds around the base. In the genus *Geranium*, after the flower has opened, the outer whorl of stamens bursts open, followed by the inner whorl. The stigma, which has been straight and pressed together, then bends outward and becomes receptive to pollen. After the flower is fertilized, there is rapid growth at the base of the style as the plant forms a rostrum or column. Attached to it are five awns or tails, each with its carpel, which contains a seed. The mericarps (they become mericarps after they separate from the carpel) gently separate from the base with their awns.

The plants then disperse their seed in one of three ways, depending on the species. In the first, the mericarp with its seed and awn attached is thrown clear of the rostrum and the awn becomes coiled. This coiling and uncoiling mechanism helps drive the seed into the ground. The genus *Erodium* has a somewhat similar mechanism, but the awn on the geranium seed is not plumed. For the second method, the mericarp without the awn is thrown some distance away and the awn drops off as this occurs. During the third method, the awn curls back and the seed is thrown out of the mericarp. Peter Yeo has very clear descriptions of these three mechanisms for those who want to pursue seed dispersal in greater depth. For gardeners, it is useful when collecting seed of rare or unusual species to know how the seed is dispersed. Ripe seed usually changes from a pale green to a light to dark brown, and it is difficult, sometimes impossible, to see if it has been dispersed onto soil. Placing a small paper (not plastic) envelope over the fruiting structure and fastening the opening with a paper clip helps to catch the seed before it is thrown out on the ground.

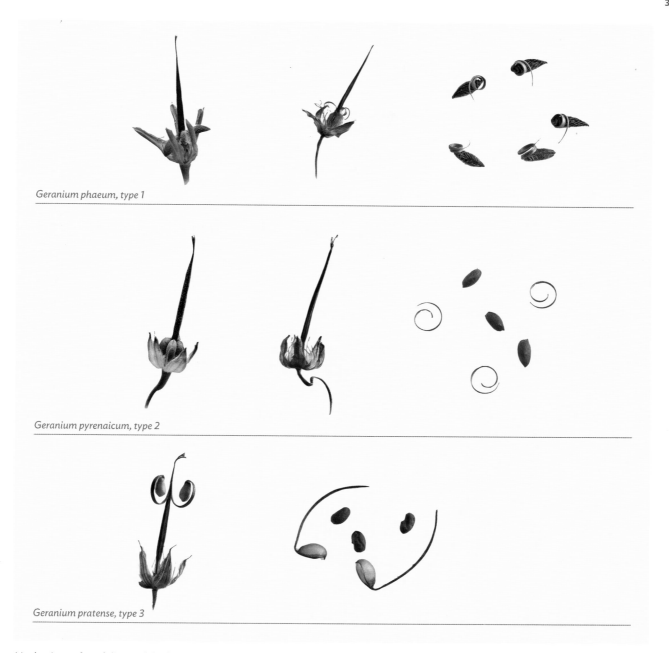

Geranium phaeum, type 1

Geranium pyrenaicum, type 2

Geranium pratense, type 3

Mechanisms of seed dispersal. In *Geranium phaeum* (top row), the mericarp with its seed and awn is thrown clear of the column and the awn becomes coiled. In *G. pyrenaicum* (middle row), the mericarp without the awn is thrown some distance away while the awn drops off. In *G. pratense* (bottom row), the awn curls back and the seed is thrown out of the mericarp.

140 HARDY GERANIUMS FOR THE GARDEN

The incomparable *Geranium* 'Rozanne' with *Prosanthera* 'Poorinda Bride' in Gary Ratway and Deborah Whigham's garden.

T

This section is organized into nine parts: Rock Gardens and Containers, Ground Covers, Shade, Scramblers and Crawlers, Borders and Bedding, Tuberous Rooted Species, Annuals, North American Species, and South African Species. These categories are not circumscribed. Generally, plants suitable for rock gardens and containers will require particular soil conditions and a certain type of light. That does not mean that plants from other sections cannot be grown in rock gardens and containers. Obviously, one would not grow a plant 5 feet (1.5 m) tall and wide in a rock garden; the perennial border would be more suitable. Look at all the different sections to see what might be suitable for your space.

The separate designations are just a starting point for thinking about placement. Geraniums in the Shade section need light shade or dappled light. Some could conceivably be grown in borders and bedding if there is a location where the plants would receive mostly light shade. Plants from the sections can also be moved around, depending on the situation in your garden. But grouping plants according to characteristics of size, growth patterns, soil and light requirements, and season of flower makes it easier to decide which plant should go where.

A number of plants listed in these pages are not easy to find, particularly at local nurseries. Even though hardy geraniums are grown and sold all over Europe and imported into the United States in the hundreds of thousands, they are still not well known because a wide range of geraniums do not appear in local suburban nurseries, and therefore remain a mystery to the general gardening public. On the west coast, there is demand for plants with long flowering cycles, and nurseries order the most basic and common geraniums, usually those that have been available for a number of years. Across the midwest and east coast, because of the climate, gardeners understand short flowering periods, but nurseries are still ordering old and well-known varieties. Recently, however, *Geranium* 'Rozanne' has promoted the awareness of hardy geraniums as good garden plants. 'Rozanne' has been sold in the millions and is justifiably popular for its stunning flowers, versatility, and adaptability to various climate challenges. The Royal Horticultural Society named it Plant of the Centenary in 2015. *Geranium* 'Brookside' and *G.* 'Orion' are quite widely used. *Geranium macrorrhizum* and *G.* ×*cantabrigiense*, particularly *G.* ×*cantabrigiense* 'Biokovo', are deservedly popular, and the Perennial Plant Association named the latter Perennial Plant of the Year for 2015. Richard Hawke, plant evaluation manager at the Chicago Botanic Garden, published an evaluation of 180 different hardy geraniums in trials at the Garden in 2012. He has done a sterling job in providing information on a wide range of these plants in a fairly rigorous climate and thus popularizing them for home gardeners.

> Hardy geraniums can be included in wild gardens, seashore gardens, small shade gardens surrounded by city buildings, and large estate gardens.

Geraniums generally look better in the garden than they do in small nursery containers, particularly when they are not in bloom. Their flowering period is usually limited to the season, either spring or summer. Relatively few flower through the three seasons of spring, summer, and fall. To see the full range of what is available in North America, it may be necessary to go plant hunting at botanic garden sales or specialty nurseries, or to ask a local nursery to order plants from a large wholesale company with a longer list. It is also possible to order seed of geranium species from plant societies, such as the Geraniaceae Group in the United Kingdom. Membership is required, but the seed list is long and full of interest.

A number of gardeners collect and grow hardy geraniums. They belong to societies such as The Hardy Plant Society or The Alpine Garden Society, which have seed lists. The most enthusiastic collectors obtain an Import Permit to bring plants and seeds into the United States, and go collecting through the nurseries of Europe. There is a fraternity of gardeners who have waited patiently to obtain plant importation permits, visited countless nurseries in out-of-the-way places, driven in rented cars loaded up to the roof with the spoils, washed plants in hotel bathrooms, and spent time with the agriculture inspectors at the airport long after the other passengers have gone home. Has it been worth it? Of course.

The breeder and the introducer of the plant, where known, are listed in this section. Most of the information is taken from *Register of Geranium Cultivar Names*, published by the Geraniaceae Group in the United Kingdom and compiled by David Victor,

Geranium ×cantabrigiense
'Berggarten'

the registrar. Many of the introductions took place in the last 15 years of the 20th century and the first 10 years of this one, and in great part in the United Kingdom. The late Peter Yeo of Cambridge University Botanic Garden deserves a great deal of credit for popularizing hardy geraniums. His *Hardy Geraniums* has been published in two editions, and is absolutely indispensable in identifying and learning about the various species. There have been new introductions of geranium cultivars and hybrids from North America, but only a few in comparison. Perhaps as geraniums are planted in more gardens, additional species and cultivars will be selected and promoted. Admittedly, some species have been overloaded with cultivars, and it is necessary to be severe in the selection process. However, the main criteria is to see what you like and to experiment.

This section is divided into a number of categories.

PLANT NAME The plant name is written in botanical Latin. There is no common name given for each species. *Geranium sanguineum* is called bloody cranesbill, but in some circles that sounds like a curse, and it is not readily obvious when you look at the plant where the name came from. The best guess is that the leaves turn red in fall, but there are a number of geraniums whose leaves do that. The meadow cranesbill, *G. pratense*, does grow in meadows, but also on hillsides and beside ditches and streams, and other geraniums grow in the same conditions. Garden writers sometimes make up common names, but gardeners tend not to use them. It is much more precise to use the botanical name.

DESCRIPTION Following the plant name is a brief description of foliage, mounding habit, flowers, and size. Usually the first thing one notices about a geranium are the flowers, including their color, size, and quantity. Flowers are often limited to one season; relatively few selections bloom from spring through fall. Many geraniums make mounds in the garden. They often have a basal rosette of leaves and flowering stems that extend above the leaves, complete with flowering stem leaves that are often smaller and with fewer lobes than the basal leaves. Some geraniums have very distinctive leaves, such as the dinner plate–size foliage of *Geranium maderense* and the brilliant yellow leaves of *G.* 'Sandrine'. Other geraniums, by virtue of their size and spread, command attention, such as *G.* 'Tiny Monster' or diminutive *G. sanguineum* 'Droplet'.

ZONES A full description of USDA Plant Hardiness Zones appears on page 247. These zones refer to minimum and maximum winter temperatures, so it is necessary to know your zone in order to choose appropriate plants.

PLANT SIZE Plant size is listed for placement purposes. Quality of soil, amount of water, and situation influence how big or small a plant grows in any garden.

SOIL Geraniums usually tolerate a wide range of soils, but you will obtain the best results with good drainage. In some cases it is important that the soil be acidic or alkaline, but soils with a slightly acidic to neutral to slightly alkaline pH will work fine. The University of Chicago Botanic Garden tests were all carried out on slightly alkaline soil with little adverse effect.

LIGHT Geraniums need enough light to flower well. If a sun geranium is planted in shade, flowering will usually decrease and the plant may look floppy and unhealthy and be vulnerable to disease. Most plants listed need morning sun, although the plants in the Shade section will grow best in a couple of hours of sun, dappled light, or light shade. Only certain geraniums need or will tolerate warm afternoon sun, particularly in hot summer gardens. But gardeners are always confounded by plants. The garden designer lists show that not everyone regards certain geraniums as shade plants, and some shade geraniums can be grown in sun. The easiest way to evaluate whether the geranium should be in sun or shade is to try it in morning sun, see how it flowers over a season, and then move it into more or less sun as needed.

PROPAGATION A separate section explains propagation of hardy geraniums (see page 232), but the suggestions on the list are quite general. Seed or some form of plant division is a suitable way to propagate the species. Seed of cultivars and hybrids will not give you the same plant, so if you selected a plant for flower color and size, for example, do vegetative propagation only for the cultivars and hybrids.

ORIGIN In the case of hybrids, this includes parentage, if known. The mere proximity of possible parents in the garden does not necessarily make children, so there is always a doubt, unless the DNA is analyzed. In the case of deliberate hybridization, the parents are definitively named. Geranium species are found in most countries of the world, and sometimes their habitat is known. It is always helpful to know where the plant was collected, but geraniums are amazingly adaptable, and they can flourish in situations quite alien to their original homes. Many of the hybrid geraniums, or the selected cultivars, originated in the United Kingdom and the Netherlands. Germany, the Netherlands, and the United Kingdom have a great tradition of plant collectors, gardeners, and nurseries that produce rare and unusual plants, and hardy geraniums

Geranium 'Mavis Simpson' in a California perennial garden.

flourish in the Zone 8 moderately cold winters and mild summers there. This is the cradle of gerani-mania.

GARDEN AND DESIGN USES Not every gardener has elaborate perennial and shrub borders. A garden may be on a balcony or a rooftop, or clustered in a group of containers. There are a number of geraniums suitable for containers, and if there is sufficient sun, they will thrive in troughs and rock gardens. Hardy geraniums can be included in wild gardens, seashore gardens, small shade gardens surrounded by city buildings, and large estate gardens. They lend themselves to plantings en masse, as well as what Michael Barclay called "glorious drifts of one."

NOTES These are helpful hints for cultivation that come from long experience growing the plants. For example, there is a note on flowering in *Geranium maderense*. So far, gardeners don't understand what triggers bloom, and some gardeners have waited up to seven years. There is a note on cutting off the flowering stems of *G. sylvaticum*, which will not reflower. Not every plant requires a note.

SUBSPECIES, VARIETIES, OR FORMS Botanists like to rank plants of the same species according to how many elements that they have in common and how they differ from each other. Subspecies, varieties, and forms differentiate plants in a particular species. They are usually not of great importance to the gardener, although flower color would certainly be of interest.

Subspecies (subsp.) have elements in common with the species but enough characteristics to differentiate them. For example, in *Geranium tuberosum*, the three middle divisions of the basal leaves are free to the base or nearly so, but divisions of the basal leaves are completely separated in *G. tuberosum* subsp. *linearifolium* and the first pair of stem leaves does not have branches. In *G. ibericum*, hairs on the pedicels separate the species into subspecies. In *G. cataractarum*, flower color and rounded leaf lobes separate the subspecies from the species.

Varieties (var.) also separate plants within their species, but at a lower level. Plants may be different from their species, but not distinct enough to be a subspecies. *Geranium sanguineum* var. *striatum* is smaller and more prostrate than the species, and the flower color is pink rather than pink-magenta.

Forms (f.) show smaller differences than a variety or subspecies. For example, *Geranium pyrenaicum* f. *albiflorum* has white flowers instead of pink ones.

Subspecies, varieties, and forms that include a full entry elsewhere in the book are listed by name only; all others include a description.

CULTIVARS These are selected cultivated forms of the different species and hybrids. When looking at the different species, it is obvious that some have a great many cultivars, such as *Geranium sanguineum*, *G. pratense*, *G. phaeum*, and *G. ×oxonianum*. There are almost certainly too many. One person is not expected to remember 90 different forms of *G. ×oxonianum* accurately. The purpose of these lists is to select the most unusual and most successful selections without being too exclusive. Cultivars that include a full entry elsewhere in the book are listed by name only; all others include a description.

HYBRIDS There have been some highly successful naturally occurring hybrids, including *Geranium ×cantabrigiense* 'Biokovo', *G.* 'Johnson's Blue', and *G. ×magnificum*. Alan Bremner in the Orkney Islands in the far north of the United Kingdom has been breeding hardy geraniums for a number of years, and he has tried many different combinations of hardy geraniums involving multiple crosses, some of which have made their way into commercial production. A number of nurseries, particularly in the Netherlands, have tried to hybridize hardy geraniums, particularly *G. wallichianum*, and some are hoping to duplicate the success of *G.* 'Rozanne'. Hybrids that include a full entry elsewhere in the book are listed by name only; all others include a description.

The following lists contain selections of hardy geraniums. These lists do not represent all the geraniums currently available. The choices are somewhat idiosyncratic, and are based on the relative ease with which the plants can be obtained and cultivated. A few are difficult, such as *Geranium* 'Nora Bremner', which is hard to find and to propagate but very beautiful, and thus worth the challenge. Of course, any number of geraniums will not suit or even thrive in every garden. Consider the lists a starting point, or an appetizer to get you started on the path to geranium delirium.

This highly unusual red-flowered and as-yet-unnamed geranium makes a useful rock garden plant.

ROCK GARDENS AND CONTAINERS

A number of hardy geraniums require sharp drainage and gritty, rocky, or sandy soil. They will flourish in rock-garden conditions or in troughs and containers. Most of them require at least a half-day of sun, except in areas with high summer temperatures, where some protection is desirable. Growing the plants in a lean, well-drained mix enables them to stay compact and live longer. Tall containers allow some alpine geraniums the long root development that many of them need to grow successfully.

Geranium ×antipodeum

A large mound of basal leaves that are slightly smaller than those of *G. traversii*. It has long, trailing, much-branched inflorescences. The leaves are green or green flushed with brown. The flowers are generally small, ¾ inch (1.9 cm) and under, and pink or white.

ZONES 8–10
PLANT SIZE 12 × 18 in. (30 × 45 cm)
SOIL Well-moistened and drained sandy or loamy soils, neutral to slightly acidic
LIGHT Full sun in mild summer gardens, morning sun and afternoon shade in hot summer gardens
PROPAGATION Basal stem cuttings
ORIGIN *G. sessiliflorum* × *G. traversii*. This plant arises in gardens when the two parents are together or where the cross is fertile. All plants from these associations are given the name *G. ×antipodeum*.
GARDEN AND DESIGN USES Walkways, edgings for borders, containers
NOTES Many different forms exist, and not all have cultivar names. Even some named cultivars look very similar.
CULTIVARS
G. ×antipodeum **'Chocolate Candy'**
G. ×antipodeum **'Pink Spice'** ▶ 8 × 12 in. (20 × 30 cm). Originally from the Lambley Nursery, Australia, in 1997. It was raised in New Zealand through repeated selection, and 'Pink Spice' was the final version. It grows as a low and dense mound. Its leaves have a satin finish and are dark brown, though they remain more green-brown if not exposed to strong light. The flowers are light pink.
G. ×antipodeum **'Stanhoe'** 6 × 24 in. (15 × 60 cm). The original 'Stanhoe' came from the garden of Ken Beckett, at Stanhoe, United Kingdom, in 1979, but the hybrid has been re-created many times. It has green leaves and pale pink flowers.
G. **'Dusky Crûg'**

Geranium ×*antipodeum* '**Chocolate Candy**' ▲

Forms a mound of large chocolate-colored leaves that are broadly dissected for half their length with widely toothed margins. The stems are dusky pink and the flowers are pale pink.

ZONES 8–10
PLANT SIZE 12–15 × 15 in. (30–38 × 38 cm)
SOIL Well-drained, acidic to neutral to alkaline
LIGHT Morning sun and afternoon shade in all but the mildest summer gardens
PROPAGATION Basal stem cuttings
ORIGIN Coen Jansen found this growing among seedlings around a plant of *G.* ×*antipodeum* 'Stanhoe' in Jansen Vaste Planten, Netherlands; he published it in 1994. Dan Heims named it.
GARDEN AND DESIGN USES In containers, on the top of rock walls, and as an edging in gardens. If you are growing it in the garden, do not overwater with an irrigation system.
NOTES You can cut it back to a few inches above the crown and it will regrow and reflower. It is, however, a short-lived perennial and should be frequently repropagated. This is a lovely plant and one of the best *G.* ×*antipodeum* selections.

Geranium argenteum

Mounds of deeply five- to seven-lobed leaves that are
further divided into three segments; silvery, silky-haired
on long gray stems. The flowers are pale pink to white
with pink-orange anthers, with purple veins, 1 inch
(2.5 cm) wide.

ZONES 7–9
PLANT SIZE 6 × 12 in. (15 × 30 cm)
SOIL Well-drained but lightly moist alkaline soil, amended
with crushed rock or gravel
LIGHT Full sun in mild summer gardens; does not tolerate
heat and humidity
PROPAGATION Cuttings of growing points, roots, seeds
(the plant seeds only occasionally)
ORIGIN In the French Alps, Hautes Alps, and Basses Alps.
In Italy, South Tyrol, and the Etruscan Apennines. In Croatia, the Julian Alps. It is found growing on cliffs and in
alpine meadows at 5500 to 7200 feet (1676–2195 m).
GARDEN AND DESIGN USES Rock gardens, alpine troughs
NOTES Crosses easily with *G. cinereum*; take care when
using seeds from the plant. It is not the easiest geranium
to maintain in cultivation. It requires perfect drainage and
readily succumbs to winter damp, but it is a very handsome plant in flower and worth the trouble if grown in the
right situation.

HYBRIDS

Geranium ×*lindavicum* **'Apple Blossom'** ▶ Parentage
possibly *G. argenteum* × *G. subcaulescens*, although it was
originally described as a *G. cinereum* cultivar. 6 × 12 in.
(15 × 30 cm). Introduced by Blooms of Bressingham,
United Kingdom, in 1969. It is a mounding plant with beautiful silvery leaves whose lobes are cut almost to the base.
The flowers are upward facing and palest pink with dark
purple veins. It grows best in Zones 7–9, in soil that is
well-drained, alkaline, and amended with gravel or perlite.
It is easy to grow if it has perfect drainage.

Geranium 'Bertie Crûg'

A wide, spreading, flattish, pancake-like plant with dark brown-pink quarter-size leaves that are rounded and scalloped. It has small, vivid, deep pink flowers that grow ¾ inch (1.9 cm) across.

ZONES 8–9; does not appear to be winter hardy in cold and wet areas
PLANT SIZE 4 × 24–36 in. (10 × 60–90 cm)
SOIL Well-drained and moist to somewhat dryish, slightly acidic to neutral to slightly alkaline
LIGHT Full sun in the very mildest summer gardens, morning sun and afternoon shade in all others

PROPAGATION Stem cuttings
ORIGIN 'Bertie Crûg' was a chance seedling (possibly *G. ×antipodeum Crûg strain × G. papuanum*) at Crûg Farm Plants in Wales in 1996, and was named after the late lamented family terrier. The dog had the ability to size up nursery visitors at a glance and treat them accordingly.
GARDEN AND DESIGN USES Most successful in raised beds with excellent drainage. It might be possible to use it in a rock garden, or as a ground cover in well-drained soil.
NOTES Does not grow well in areas of high summer heat and humidity. It flowers in late spring; you can cut it back for a second flowering in fall.

Geranium Cinereum Group

Low-growing mounds with finger-like branches that are covered with old brown stipules. Leaves at the tips have a rounded outline with small lobes or are dissected almost to the base. The leaves are silver-gray, gray, or gray-green. They grow long, single, or paired flowering stems from the root stock and become covered with flowers from late spring to early summer. Flowers range in color from white through pale pink to medium pink to magenta, often with prominent veins and blotches. Flowers 1–1½ in. (2.5–3.8 cm).

ZONES 5–9

PLANT SIZE 6–12 × 8–15 in. (15–30 × 20–38 cm)

SOIL Well-drained, preferably amended with sand or grit; the plants seem to prefer an alkaline soil, although they will grow in slightly acidic to neutral

LIGHT Morning sun and afternoon shade in mild summer gardens only

PROPAGATION Tip cuttings; plants are difficult to divide by the roots because they have a single large root system

ORIGIN This group occurs in the Atlas Mountains of Morocco (*G. cinereum* subsp. *nanum*), in southeast and northern Spain, in the Pyrenees, French Alps (*G. argenteum*), Apennines, eastern Italian Alps (*G. argenteum*), Balkan Peninsula, Turkey and Greece (*G. subcaulescens*), Transcaucasia, Syria, and Lebanon. Others, like *G. ×lindavicum*, apparently originally occurred in gardens.

GARDEN AND DESIGN USES These are rock garden and container plants, but you can also grow them in a well-drained area in the front of a border, over a rock wall, or between stepping stones. They will not tolerate traffic, however.

NOTES This group is sensitive to summer heat and humidity. In high summer temperatures these plants do not grow well or for a long period of time, and they may survive for a only couple of years before dying. If you cut back plants after flowering, they will releaf and reflower.

CULTIVARS

G. (Cinereum Group) 'Alice' 6 × 12 in. (15 × 30 cm). Bred by Carl and Janette Lowe of Border Alpines, United Kingdom, published in 1998, and named after Carl's mother. Gray-green leaves and pale lilac-pink flowers.

G. (Cinereum Group) 'Carol' ◄ 6 × 10 in. (15 × 25 cm). Carl and Janette Lowe created this and named it after one of their friends. It has large bright pink flowers with deeper reddish centers and purple veins.

G. (Cinereum Group) 'Lizabeth' 6 × 10 in. (15 × 25 cm). Carl Lowe introduced this in 1999. It grows pale pink flowers with light purple veins and gray-green leaves.

G. (Cinereum Group) 'Purple Pillow' ► 6 × 12 in. (15 × 30 cm). From Bridgemere Nurseries, United Kingdom, in 2000.

The flowers are red-purple with dark veins and an almost black center. The leaves are blue-green.

G. (Cinereum Group) 'Queen of Hearts' 6 × 10 in. (15 × 25 cm). From Cyril Foster in the United Kingdom, and marketed by Blooms of Bressingham. White flowers with dark veins, a pink center, and yellow-green stamens.

G. (Cinereum Group) 'Rothbury Gem' ▲ 5 × 14 in. (12.5 × 36 cm). From Cyril Foster, United Kingdom, marketed by Blooms of Bressingham. Flowers are light pink with deep magenta-pink veins and a deep pink center. Leaves are gray-green.

G. (Cinereum Group) 'Signal' 8 × 12 in. (20 × 30 cm). From the Sarastro Nursery, Austria, in 1999. Eugen Schleipfer, Augsburg, Germany, raised this. It has vivid magenta flowers.

G. (Cinereum Group) 'Thumbling Hearts' ▶ (also known as 'Thumping Hearts', but due to an error in registration the former name has precedence) 6 × 12 in. (15 × 30 cm). Hybridized in the Netherlands by Hubertus Gerardus, Oudshoorn, and introduced in 2009 by Future Plants. The flowers have a pale lavender background with magenta veins and dark magenta-purple blotches that take up at least half of the flower. The flowers are slightly cupped and the edges are irregular. The leaves are gray-green.

G. 'Memories' 8 × 12 in. (20 × 30 cm). A chance seedling Carl Lowe found in his nursery in the United Kingdom in 1999 and named in memory of Aad Zoet. The leaves are gray-green and deeply lobed. The flowers are purple-red with prominent dark purple veins and a small white ring at the base. The leaves have good fall color.

G. 'Sateene' 8 × 15 in. (20 × 38 cm). Carl Lowe found this at his nursery in the United Kingdom in 1999. Red-purple flowers with dark veins. Flowers appear satiny in certain lights. It has a long flowering period, from late spring to late summer.

HYBRIDS

G. (Cinereum Group) 'Ballerina' ▶ Parentage uncertain. 8 × 15 in. (20 × 38 cm). From Blooms of Bressingham, United Kingdom, in 1963. The flowers have a pale lavender-pink background with dark purple-red veins.

G. (Cinereum Group) 'Lambrook' Possible parentage *G. cinereum* var. *subcaulescens* × *G. cinereum* var. *obtusifolium,* seedling. 8 × 12 in. (20 × 30 cm). Features pale veins on cold pink flowers that become whiter toward the center.

G. (Cinereum Group) 'Laurence Flatman' ▶ Parentage *G.* (Cinereum Group) 'Ballerina' × *G. cinereum* var. *subcaulescens*. 8 × 15 in. (20 × 38 cm). From Blooms of Bressingham, United Kingdom, in 1979. This was named after the nursery foreman, who raised it. The flowers have a very pale lavender-pink background, with veins and a center that are dark red-purple, and light purple blotches on all five petals.

Geranium 'Dusky Crûg'

An attractive mound of light green-brown five-lobed leaves with very pale lavender-pink flowers.

PLANT SIZE 8–10 × 15 in. (20–25 × 38 cm)
ZONES 7–9
SOIL Well-drained loam, slightly acidic to neutral
LIGHT Morning sun and afternoon shade in hot summer gardens, full sun in mild summer gardens
PROPAGATION Crown division
ORIGIN Possibly *G. ×antipodeum Crûg* strain × *G. ×oxonianum*. Found in the nursery at Crûg Farm Plants, Wales.
GARDEN AND DESIGN USES An attractive front-of-border accent in mild summer gardens, containers
NOTES If grown in sufficient sun the leaves are brownish, but take care to regulate the length of summer sun, as the leaves are inclined to burn in hot sun. The plant seeds readily, as do all the *G. ×antipodeum* selections and crosses. Remove seedlings ruthlessly.

Geranium 'Elizabeth Ross'

Forms a low spreading mound of five-lobed gray-green leaves with magenta flowers on short stems. Blooms throughout the summer.

ZONES 7–9

PLANT SIZE 8 × 36 in. (20 × 90 cm)

SOIL Well-drained loam, slightly acidic to neutral

LIGHT Morning sun/afternoon shade in hot summer gardens, full sun in mild summer gardens

PROPAGATION Crown division

ORIGIN *G. ×antipodeum* × *G. ×oxonianum*. Alan Bremner hybridized this and named it after the wife of John Ross, of the former Charter House Nursery.

GARDEN AND DESIGN USES Rock gardens, containers

Geranium farreri

A dwarf alpine plant forming small mounds of 2-inch (5 cm) wide leaves that are divided into five to seven lobes, which themselves are divided into three or more lobes. The leaves are faintly marbled and their edges are toothed. It has a thick and long taproot, and pale pink flowers a little more than 1 inch (2.5 cm) in diameter, with light green veins, a white center, and green bracts. The anthers are a prominent blue-black.

ZONES 5–8
PLANT SIZE 5–8 × 12 in. (12.5–20 × 30 cm)
SOIL Shale or limestone scree, sandy or chalky, alkaline
LIGHT Full sun in mild summer gardens
PROPAGATION Seed; plants form taproots that are quite difficult to divide
ORIGIN Found in northwestern China, Gansu Province, near Tibet and Sichuan
GARDEN AND DESIGN USES Rock garden, alpine trough
NOTES Quite difficult to grow and maintain in hot summer gardens.

Geranium 'Luscious Linda'

A low mound of bronze-green leaves with long trailing stems. The flowers are small and strong mauve-lilac with a small white center.

ZONES 8–9
PLANT SIZE 6–8 × 20 in. (15–20 × 50 cm)
SOIL Well-drained moderate loam, slightly acidic to neutral
LIGHT Full sun in mild summer gardens; leaves can burn in hot afternoon sun
PROPAGATION Restricted to licensed propagators
ORIGIN A form of *G. ×antipodeum*. From Richard Rendall at Tranquility Gardens, (Orkney Perennials) St. Ola, Orkney Islands, United Kingdom, in 2005.
GARDEN AND DESIGN USES Edging for a perennial border, rock garden, containers
NOTES Originally described as having green leaves, but current plants have bronze-green foliage. You can cut back the plant to 3 inches (7.5 cm) above the crown to refresh the leaves and produce more flowers.

Geranium nanum

A compact small plant with deep green small, rounded leaves with shallow lobes. The white flowers have purple to colorless veins and notched petals and are 0.9 inch (2.3 cm) in diameter. It blooms in late spring and is long flowering. Charles Aitchison saw it in habitat growing in scree over red clay. It is, he says, "a plant of late snow melt beds in association with a number of other rare plants."

ZONES 5–9
PLANT SIZE 4 × 8 in. (10 × 20 cm)
SOIL Scree, neutral to alkaline
LIGHT Sun
PROPAGATION Seed, stem cuttings
ORIGIN According to Peter Yeo, this comes from one isolated locality in the Atlas Mountains of Morocco.
GARDEN AND DESIGN USES Rock garden, trough, containers
NOTES Greatest success in cultivating this plant has been reported in areas where there is dry snow cover during the winter.
HYBRIDS Hybridizes with *G. subcaulescens*, but the progeny are not named.

Geranium 'Orkney Cherry'

Forms a mound with trailing stems of bronze-green small, rounded, deeply lobed leaves. It grows deep cherry-pink flowers with white throats and purple veins during a long flowering period, from May until frost.

ZONES 8–10
PLANT SIZE 10 × 24 in. (25 × 60 cm)
SOIL Well-drained medium moist loam, neutral to alkaline
LIGHT Full sun in mild summer gardens
PROPAGATION Restricted to licensed propagators
ORIGIN *G.* ×*antipodeum* × *G.* ×*oxonianum*. Alan Bremner, Orkney Islands, United Kingdom, hybridized this and named it for the islands.
GARDEN AND DESIGN USES Perennial borders, rock garden, containers, cottage gardens
NOTES Finding the right place in the garden is important to ensure the success of this plant. Too much sun and it will burn; too little sun and it will not flower properly. It does not tolerate high heat and humidity. Shear to 3 inches (7.5 cm) above the crown to refresh for new leaves and flowers. 'Orkney Pink' (possibly *G.* ×*antipodeum* × *G.* ×*oxonianum*), raised before 1994 by Alan Bremner, is similar but has soft medium pink flowers with a white eye.

Geranium sessiliflorum

Forms a pancake mound with a central rootstock and long spreading stems. The rounded, deeply lobed, and slighted indented leaves are green in the South American and Australian plants, and varying shades of brown in New Zealand. The flowers are white or very pale pink, about ½ inch (1.25 cm) across. They grow at the heads of the flowering stems and are held at the level of the foliage.

ZONES 8–10

PLANT SIZE 3–5 × 12–15 in. (7.5–12.5 × 30–38 cm)

SOIL Well-drained, rocky to gravelly with some loam, slightly acidic to neutral to alkaline

LIGHT Full sun in mild summer gardens, morning sun and afternoon shade in hot summer gardens

PROPAGATION Stems, seed

ORIGIN It is native to Australasia, and found in New Zealand, Tasmania, and the South Eastern Highlands of Australia. It is also found in Argentina, Bolivia, and Chile. It grows in alpine grasslands, scree, and rock from sea level up to 16,000 feet (4875 m). Three forms are distinguished: *G. sessiliflorum* subsp. *novaezelandiae*, *G. sessiliflorum* subsp. *sessiliflorum*, and *G. sessiliflorum* subsp. *brevicaule*. The cultivated plants for gardens are from subsp. *novaezelandiae* and its hybrids.

GARDEN AND DESIGN USES Rock garden, trough, gravel path

NOTES *G. sessiliflorum* seeds profusely, particularly into gravel. Take care to place it where it will not overwhelm other plants. It has hybridized with a second New Zealand species *G. traversii* to make *G. ×antipodeum* and has produced a wide range of seedlings of varying leaf size and color.

CULTIVARS

G. sessiliflorum subsp. novaezelandiae 'Nigricans' ▶ 5 × 12 in. (12.5 × 30 cm). Leaves are a sooty dark gray-green that may turn black in full sun. They become orange when stressed or about to die. Flowers are white.

G. sessiliflorum subsp. novaezelandiae 'Porters Pass' 5 × 12 in. (12.5 × 30 cm). Its leaves are red-brown and the flowers are white. The plants seem to come true from seed.

HYBRIDS

G. ×antipodeum

G. 'Libretto' Parentage *G. sessiliflorum* subsp. *novaezelandiae* 'Nigricans' × *G. lambertii* 'Swansdown'. 12–15 × 18 in. (30–38 × 45 cm). Forms a large mound of light brown leaves with small white flowers. Grow this plant for the foliage. An Alan Bremner hybrid from Catforth Gardens, United Kingdom, in 1993.

Geranium subcaulescens

A mound of sage green small, rounded, five- to seven-lobed, dissected leaves. The flowers are brilliant magenta with black centers on long flowering stems. Flowers are 1 inch (2.5 cm).

ZONES 7–9
PLANT SIZE 8–10 × 15 in. (20–25 × 38 cm)
SOIL Well-drained, gritty or sandy soil, alkaline
LIGHT Full sun in mild summer gardens; does not do well in heat and humidity
PROPAGATION Short stem cuttings, seed of the species only
ORIGIN Turkey, Albania, Greece, and the Balkans. Alpine areas.

GARDEN AND DESIGN USES Rock gardens, troughs, front of a perennial border with adequate drainage
CULTIVARS
G. subcaulescens **'Splendens'** 7 × 12 in. (18 × 30 cm). This was thought to be an old cultivar that George Arends raised in Germany in the 1930s, although the records were lost in the war and other nurseries also claimed to have propagated it. The name and the plant are confused in the nursery trade, as plants sold in North America under this name are actually *G. subcaulescens*. 'Splendens' has bright salmon-pink flowers that have very small white blotches at the base of the petals and dark brown-black centers. The petals are slightly reflexed.

Geranium 'Tanya Rendall'

A low-growing mound of purple-bronze, seven-lobed, small, round leaves that mature to dark bronze-green. Its flowers are vivid dark pink with a white eye and prominent veins.

ZONES 8–10
PLANT SIZE 6 × 18 in. (15 × 45 cm)
SOIL Well-drained loam, slightly acidic to neutral
LIGHT Full sun in mild summer gardens, morning sun and afternoon shade in hot summer gardens
PROPAGATION Restricted to licensed propagators.
ORIGIN G. ×antipodeum 'Black Ice' × G. ×oxonianum cultivar. Tranquility Cottage Nursery, St. Ola, Orkney Islands, United Kingdom, raised this in 2005 as part of a planned breeding program to develop plants for hanging baskets and garden use.
GARDEN AND DESIGN USES Good edging for a border, containers
NOTES The plant will burn up in hot summer sun. Site it carefully so the leaves remain brown without burning. Flowers for a long period during the spring and summer.

Geranium traversii

A mounding plant with long stems supporting silver-gray leaves with seven lobes. The lobes are overlapping, rounded, broad, shallow, and toothed. The flowers are white on long flowering stems, ¾ inch (1.9 cm) in diameter, and saucer shaped.

ZONES 9–10
PLANT SIZE 12 × 24 in. (30 × 60 cm)
SOIL Sandy soil to loam, moist, well-drained, slightly acidic to neutral
LIGHT Full sun in mild summer gardens
PROPAGATION Roots, crowns, seed
ORIGIN From New Zealand's Chatham Islands. Grows on coastal cliffs.
GARDEN AND DESIGN USES Front of a perennial border, containers
NOTES Intolerant of summer heat and winter cold. If you lose the plant, you can easily propagate it from seed.
VARIETIES
G. traversii var. elegans ▲ 12 × 18 in. (30 × 45 cm). A pink-flowered form. Flowers fade to pale pink around the edges.
HYBRIDS
G. ×antipodeum
G. 'Joy'
G. ×riversleaianum

GROUND COVERS

Many ground covers are plants with innumerable crowns whose roots extend through the ground. Some spread more aggressively than others and are better suited for large areas. Most ground-covering plants tolerate morning sun and afternoon shade and do best in light shade or areas with filtered light. They are effective as underplantings for trees and shrubs, as well as for suppressing weeds in otherwise bare areas that are hard to cultivate. In addition to colorful flowers, they offer varied foliage shapes and hues. The plants listed in these pages represent the most distinctive cultivars currently available in North America.

Geranium ×cantabrigiense

Forms dense mats of slender, long, woody brown stems above ground. It has thin roots with many growing points below ground. The leaves are palmate, five-lobed, shiny, almost hairless, and about 1½ inches (3.8 cm) in diameter, and they have a light fragrance. The flowers are pink and 1 inch (2.5 cm) in diameter.

ZONES 4–10

PLANT SIZE 9 × 20 in. (23 × 50 cm)

SOIL Well-drained to dry, slightly alkaline to neutral to mildly acidic soil

LIGHT Light shade; leaves become yellowish with too much hot summer sun

PROPAGATION Root division

ORIGIN *G. macrorrhizum* × *G. dalmaticum*. Helen Kiefer experimentally raised this at Cambridge University Botanic Garden and ultimately gave it the name 'Cambridge'.

GARDEN DESIGN AND USES *G. ×cantabrigiense* is one of the most widely used geraniums in gardens. It is a spreading ground cover for borders, shade gardens, large public spaces, and even large containers. There are numerous named cultivar selections.

NOTES Flowers heavily in the spring and to a far lesser degree in fall as the weather cools. It has no flowers in the summer, but retains its green leaves throughout winter. The plant can be invasive, so site it where you can easily remove it. Even small pieces can regenerate, so be sure removal is thorough. It is not recommended for rock gardens. It is drought tolerant when established.

CULTIVARS

G. ×cantabrigiense **'Berggarten'** ◀ 9 × 18 in. (23 × 45 cm). From Gartnerei Simon, Germany, in the mid-1990s, and distributed by Axletree Nursery, United Kingdom, in 1997. It has bright medium pink flowers.

G. ×cantabrigiense **'Biokovo'** ▼ 9 × 20 in. (23 × 50 cm). Hans Simon collected this in Biokovo, Croatia, and his nursery, Gartnerei Simon, Germany, distributed it in 1980. The flowers are white with rusty pink streaks as they age. This is probably the most widely grown of all *G. ×cantabrigiense*. The Perennial Plant Association in the United States named it 2015 Perennial Plant of the Year.

***G.* ×*cantabrigiense* 'Cambridge'** ▲ 9 × 20 in. (23 × 50 cm). The buds are almost red, the flowers are light pink, and the leaves have good reddish fall color.

***G.* ×*cantabrigiense* 'Crystal Rose'** ▶ 8 × 15 in. (20 × 38 cm). Selected in the Netherlands from *G.* ×*cantabrigiense* 'Westray'. It has hot pink flowers, and is in bloom from early summer to fall. Leaves are small, shiny, and broadly lobed, and they have an orange color in fall if temperatures are low enough. The flowers are profuse and are held well above the leaves. A license is required for propagation.

G. ×*cantabrigiense* 'Hanne' ◄ 8 × 20 in. (20 × 50 cm). From Denmark. It has soft pink flowers with a pale, almost white, edge to the petals.

G. ×*cantabrigiense* 'Harz' ▲ 8 × 18 in. (20 × 45 cm). From Sarastro Nursery, Austria, in 2001. Herr Fuss of Königslutter, Germany, raised it. Flowers are almost white.

G. ×*cantabrigiense* 'Jans' 10 × 50 in. (25 × 127 cm). Described from Geranium Trial Results at The Chicago Botanic Garden. White flowers with a pink blush.

G. ×*cantabrigiense* 'Karmina' 9 × 20 in. (23 × 50 cm). Ernst Pagels of Germany raised this. It was, at one time, a little darker pink than *G.* ×*cantabrigiense* 'Cambridge', but seems to have been mixed up with 'Cambridge' in the nursery trade. The two now are often interchangeable in color.

G. ×*cantabrigiense* 'Vorjura' 9 × 20 in. (23 × 50 cm). It has medium pink flowers with white veins and a white center.

HYBRIDS

G. ×***cantabrigiense* 'St. Ola'** Parentage *G. dalmaticum* 'Album' × *G. macrorrhizum* 'Album'. 8 × 20 in. (20 × 50 cm). Alan Bremner, Orkney Islands, United Kingdom, hybridized this, and Axletree Nursery, United Kingdom, distributed it in 1993. It has creamy white flowers that have a pink tint as they age, and deep green leaves that are somewhat flatter than those of *G.* ×*cantabrigiense* 'Biokovo'.

G. ×***cantabrigiense* 'Westray'** ▼ (*G. macrorrhizum* 'Lohfelden' × *G. dalmaticum*) 8 × 20 in. (20 × 50 cm). Alan Bremner, Orkney Islands, United Kingdom, hybridized this. It has dark pink flowers, and the leaves are smaller than those of *G.* ×*cantabrigiense* 'Cambridge'. It was named after one of the Orkney Islands.

Geranium dalmaticum

A low-growing ground cover with small leaves, ½–1 inch (1.25–2.5 cm) in diameter, that are divided into five to seven deep lobes. Leaves have a good reddish fall color in sun. Medium pink flowers are 1 inch (2.5 cm) wide and appear in late spring.

ZONES 4–10

PLANT SIZE 5 × 24–36 in. (12.5 × 60–90 cm)

SOIL Light loam to sandy and gravel soils, well-drained, lightly acidic to neutral to slightly alkaline

LIGHT Full sun in mild summer gardens, morning sun/afternoon shade in hot summer gardens; will also grow in light shade

PROPAGATION Seed (for the species only), root division

ORIGIN Found in Croatia, Macedonia, and northern Albania, and introduced into cultivation in the United Kingdom in the 1940s.

GARDEN AND DESIGN USES Ground cover for rock gardens, between stepping stones, and shrub borders. Do not place it where it can overrun other small plants.

NOTES Will usually flower for only one month in the late spring, so plant primarily as a ground cover. It is sun tolerant but becomes very compact, down to 3 inches (7.5 cm), in strong light.

CULTIVARS

G. dalmaticum 'Album' ◄ 5 × 24–36 in. (12.5 × 60–90 cm). Blooms of Bressingham, United Kingdom, introduced this in 1956. It has white flowers that are very faintly flushed with pink as the flower ages.

G. dalmaticum 'Bridal Bouquet' ▲ 6 × 24–36 in. (15 × 60–90 cm). Slack Top Alpine Nursery, United Kingdom, raised this. The flowers feature pink veins on white petals that become pink as they age. It usually differs from *G. dalmaticum* 'Album' by being slightly taller with perkier flowers as they age.

Geranium endressii

Forms mounds of light green divided, five-lobed leaves that are attractively veined with sharply pointed leaf divisions. The flowers are a bright chalky pink when they open and become darker with age. They are 1½ inches (3.8 cm) and funnel shaped with notched petals.

ZONES 4–10
PLANT SIZE 18 × 24 in. (45 × 60 cm)
SOIL Fertile, well-drained, slightly acidic to neutral to slightly alkaline
LIGHT Morning sun and afternoon shade, light dappled shade
PROPAGATION Roots, crowns, seed
GARDEN AND DESIGN USES Useful for morning sun and afternoon shade gardens, or gardens with light dappled shade as a ground cover or a single plant.
ORIGIN Native to the French Pyrenees, extending just into Spain. It hybridizes with a number of other geraniums, including *G. versicolor* (*G.* ×*oxonianum*), *G. psilostemon*, *G. sessiliflorum*, and *G. traversii* (*G.* ×*riversleaianum*).
NOTES Makes a dense ground cover by spreading clumps

and seeding. This is not a good plant choice for the Deep South, as high humidity affects it adversely. It has passed on the changing color of its flowers to some of its hybrids.

CULTIVARS
G. endressii **'Betty Catchpole'** 18 × 24 in. (45 × 60 cm). Mauve-pink flowers, funnel shaped and with separated petals.
G. endressii **'Castle Drogo'** 15 × 24 in. (38 × 60 cm). Salmon-pink flowers.

HYBRIDS
G. **'Mary Mottram'** Parentage *G. endressii* × *G. sylvaticum* 'Album'. 12 × 18 in. (30 × 45 cm). Originally from the nursery of Mary Mottram, United Kingdom, as *G. endressii* 'Album'. It has mounds of light green leaves and flowers with vase-shaped white notched petals that change to pale pink as they age.
G. **'Melinda'** Parentage *G. endressii* × *G. sylvaticum* 'Mayflower'. 24–30 × 24 in. (60–75 × 60 cm). From Rijnbeek Nursery, Netherlands, around 2007. Foliage similar to *G. sylvaticum*. Very pale pink flowers with darker rose-pink veins.

Geranium macrorrhizum

Fleshy underground rhizomatous roots and tall, thick, leafy stems with leaves that are large, sticky, and aromatic, and have five to seven deep and rounded lobes. It has 1-inch (2.5 cm) light magenta-pink flowers that have reddish sepals and are located well above the foliage. It makes a vigorous ground cover.

ZONES 3–10

PLANT SIZE 15 × 30 in. (38 × 75 cm)

SOIL Tolerant of average soil, acidic to neutral to slightly alkaline. It increases in size more rapidly in fertile soil that is slightly, but not overly, damp.

LIGHT You can grow the plant in sun, but the leaves tend to turn yellow-green. It looks better in light to medium shade.

PROPAGATION Seed, root division. Grow the cultivars from root division, as they are selected for particular variations, flower color, and size. Grow the species from seed.

ORIGIN It is found at the eastern end of the Mediterranean, in the southern Alps, Apennines, Carpathians, and the Balkan peninsula. It grows among rocks and scrub, usually in the shade, although there have been some high-altitude collections on rocky slopes in alkaline soil.

GARDEN AND DESIGN USES The species is a weed-smothering ground cover for large areas. The species is not intended for small gardens, although some of the shorter selections, such as *G. macrorrhizum* 'Lohfelden' or *G. macrorrhizum* 'Pindus', would be suitable. Take care in planting so it does not overrun other choice plants.

NOTES If you cut it back to several inches above the crown, the plant will releaf and reflower.

CULTIVARS

G. macrorrhizum **'Album'** ▲ 15 × 40 in. (38 × 102 cm). Walter Ingwersen discovered this in the Rhodope Mountains, Bulgaria, and described it in 1946. It has medium green pungent leaves and white flowers with rusty pink calyces. The plant can look pinkish at a distance.

***G. macrorrhizum* 'Bevan's Variety'** 15 × 40 in. (38 × 102 cm). Roger Bevan collected this in the former Yugoslavia in 1961. The leaves are pungent, the flowers are red-purple, and the sepals are deep red.

***G. macrorrhizum* 'Cham Ce'** 18 × 40 in. (45 × 102 cm). Hans Simon collected this and distributed it through his nursery in Germany. It is taller than *G. macrorrhizum* and has medium pink flowers with dark pink veins and a small white eye.

***G. macrorrhizum* 'Czakor'** 12 × 36 in. (30 × 90 cm). Hans Simon collected this in the Czakor Gorge, Montenegro. It has slightly darker red-purple flowers than 'Bevan's Variety', but the two are mixed up in the nursery trade. Its calyces are green.

***G. macrorrhizum* 'Ingwersen's Variety'** ◀ 15 × 48 in. (38 × 122 cm). Walter Ingwersen described it in 1946. It was originally collected on Mount Koprivnik, Montenegro, in 1929. Although initially described as having large rose-colored flowers, the plants currently available in the nursery trade have pale pink flowers.

***G. macrorrhizum* 'Lohfelden'** 8 × 18 in. (20 × 45 cm). Heinz Klose collected this, and named it for the town in Germany where his nursery is based. It is quite a compact plant and slow growing, with small white flowers that have prominent pink veins.

G. macrorrhizum 'Pindus' 8–10 × 20 in. (20–25 × 50 cm). A. W. A. (Bill) Baker collected this in the Pindus Mountains, Greece, and Axletree Nursery, United Kingdom, described the plant in its catalog in 1993. It is noteworthy for its large, shiny green calyces and magenta-pink flowers. The plant is more compact than *G. macrorrhizum*. Because of its low height and lack of vigor, it is an attractive container plant.

G. macrorrhizum 'Ridsko' 15 × 30 in. (38 × 75 cm). Trevor Bath and Joy Jones, United Kingdom, first described this in 1994. The leaves are light green and slightly glossy. It is said to lose its leaves in the winter, but this has not been the case in mild climates. The flowers are pale magenta-pink.

G. macrorrhizum 'Rotblut' 8 × 24 in. (20 × 60 cm). A small compact form of *G. macrorrhizum* with light magenta flowers and green calyces.

G. macrorrhizum 'Spessart' 15 × 40 in. (38 × 102 cm). Hans Simon, Germany, collected this in 1955. The flowers are white and the calyces are rusty pink.

G. macrorrhizum 'Variegatum' ▲ 15 × 30 in. (38 × 75 cm). This has been in cultivation in the United Kingdom since before 1900. It has irregularly splashed cream and green variegation, and light magenta-pink flowers. It is much less vigorous than other forms of *G. macrorrhizum*, and a little more difficult to propagate.

G. macrorrhizum 'Velebit' 15 × 30 in. (38 × 75 cm). From Gartnerei Simon, Germany, in 1990. Hans Simon collected it in the Velebit Mountains, Croatia. The plant is tall, the petals are medium magenta-pink, and the calyces are small and green.

G. macrorrhizum 'White-Ness' ▶ 18–20 × 30 in. (45–50 × 75 cm). Members of the Ness Botanic Garden collected it on Mount Olympus, and Crûg Farm Plants published the plant in its catalog in 1997. It is tall, with small pure white flowers and clear medium green leaves. Useful for those who want no hint of pink in the garden.

Geranium ×oxonianum

Makes a clump-forming mound. Leaves are five-lobed and deeply dissected. Foliage shows some variation of a brown patch that is present or absent depending on the selection, a characteristic derived from one of the parents, *G. versicolor*. Flowers are funnel shaped with notched petals and come in white and many shades of pink, often with dark veins. Flower size varies between 1¼ and 1½ inches (3.1–3.8 cm). Some named cultivars also have petals that are narrow, star shaped, small, and almost double. In some selections of *G. ×oxonianum* the flowers are pale pink when young and deepen in color as they age.

ZONES 4–10

PLANT SIZE 15–24 × 18–30 in. (38–60 × 45–75 cm)

SOIL Average moist to dry medium loam, slightly acidic to neutral; tolerates some drought

LIGHT Full sun to partial shade; flower color tends to fade in full hot sun

PROPAGATION Crown division, not from seed

ORIGIN *G. endressii* × *G. versicolor*. This fertile hybrid has produced many dozens of named selections, not always readily distinguishable. There are more than 87 different named forms of *G. ×oxonianum*, and 99 percent of them are pink.

GARDEN AND DESIGN USES Perennial borders, shrub borders, containers, light shade gardens

NOTES It is important to cut back *G. ×oxonianum* selections in midseason after flowering, otherwise the plants tend to flop outward from the center and flowering decreases. It will tolerate considerable summer heat, but resents—as do many plants of this hybrid—high summer humidity and direct hot afternoon sun, which cause the large leaves to wilt and burn. Beware of the enormous number of seeds *G. ×oxonianum* produces. It seems as though every one will germinate. Cut back plants after flowering and pull up any seedlings. The stems of large-leafed and

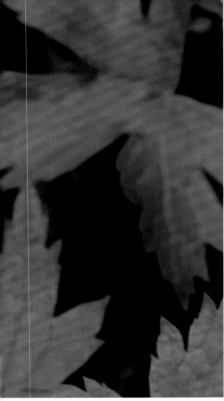

large-flowered forms of G. ×oxonianum (such as 'Claridge Druce', 'Königshof', 'Julie Brennan', G. ×oxonianum f. thurstonianum, and G. ×oxonianum f. thurstonianum 'Sherwood') grow out of the ground to an extent that impedes flowering. Every couple of years, divide these forms and replant with at least half of the stems buried.

Given the tendency of G. ×oxonianum to seed prolifically, there are innumerable versions of this hybrid. Gardeners and nursery people tend to name plants without reference to what is already available. The following list of cultivars represents the most noteworthy, but a number of others are not listed, and more are named all the time.

CULTIVARS

G. ×oxonianum 'Ankum's White' ◀ 12–15 × 18 in. (30–38 × 45 cm). From Coen Jansen, Netherlands, in 2002. Flowers are pure white with lavender veins and notched petals. The plant is quite compact.

G. ×oxonianum 'Anmore' ▼ 18 × 20 in. (45 × 50 cm). From Phoebe Noble and Rainforest Gardens, British Columbia, Canada, around 1993. The foliage is pale green and markedly different from the other G. ×oxonianum selections. Flowers are very pale silver-pink.

G. ×oxonianum 'A. T. Johnson' 18 × 24 in. (45 × 60 cm). This is a very old variety, originally published by Walter Ingwersen in 1946 and named after A. T. Johnson, who discovered it in Wales before 1937. It has luminous soft pink flowers with translucent veins. The petals have an iridescent sheen.

G. ×*oxonianum* **'Breckland Sunset'** ▲ 24 × 24 in. (60 × 60 cm). The Plantsman's Preference, United Kingdom, selected this in 1998. Flowers are deep carmine pink with carmine pink veins.

G. ×*oxonianum* **'Bregover Pearl'** ▶ 18 × 20 in. (45 × 50 cm). From Bregover Plants in Cornwall, United Kingdom, from the early 1990s. Very light pink flowers with green veins, a green center, and brown-blotched foliage.

G. *×oxonianum* **'Bressingham's Delight'** 15 × 24 in. (38 × 60 cm). Adrian Bloom, Blooms of Bressingham, United Kingdom, selected and patented this. It has soft pink flowers and a neat mounding habit.

G. *×oxonianum* **'Claridge Druce'** ◀ 30 × 36 in. (75 × 90 cm). Claridge Druce, United Kingdom, found this in 1900. It produces large mounds of medium green coarse, hairy leaves that have faint maroon internodal blotches. Flowers are light pink with purple veins that coalesce, giving the flower a dark pink appearance. It is one of the largest-flowering forms of G. ×oxonianum, along with G. ×oxonianum 'Königshof', 'Pat Smallacombe', and f. *thurstonianum*. The plant becomes very ragged by midsummer, but you can shear it to the ground to produce new leaves and flowers.

G. *×oxonianum* **'Dawn Time'** 18 × 24 in. (45 × 60 cm). Croftway Nursery, United Kingdom, introduced it in 1998. The leaves are marked with brown internodal blotches and the flowers are pale pink with prominent veins.

G. *×oxonianum* **'Elworthy Misty'** ◀ 18 × 24 in. (45 × 60 cm). From Elworthy Cottage Gardens in Somerset, United Kingdom, in 1999. It is a seedling from G. ×oxonianum 'Walter's Gift'. The leaves have strong brown markings, and the flowers are deep pink with prominent purple veins.

G. *×oxonianum* **'Frank Lawley'** 18 × 24 in. (45 × 60 cm). Robin Moss found this in the garden of Frank Lawley, Herterton House, and Axletree Nursery, United Kingdom, introduced this in 1994. It has medium green leaves and pale pink flowers.

G. ×*oxonianum* **'Fran's Star'** ▲ 24 × 36 in. (60 × 90 cm). Shiny green leaves with brown internodal blotches and small rose-pink semi-double flowers (the extra petals are petalloid stamens).

G. ×*oxonianum* **'Hollywood'** ◀ 28 × 30 in. (71 × 75 cm). Langthorn's Plantery, United Kingdom, introduced this around 1990. The leaves are hairy and marked with faint internodal blotches. It has quite large 1½-inch (3.8 cm) pale pink flowers with magenta-purple veins.

G. ×*oxonianum* **'Julie Brennan'** ▶ 18 × 24 in. (45 × 60 cm). Judith Bradshaw of Catforth Gardens, United Kingdom, introduced this in 1994. It has dark pink flowers with a network of dark purple veins.

G. ×*oxonianum* **'Juliet's Pink'** ▼ 15 × 15 in. (38 × 38 cm). Selected from the garden of Juliet Robinson, United Kingdom, in 1994 and introduced by Geraniaceae Nursery, California. It has medium green hairy leaves with faint internodal blotches and pale pink flowers with prominent purple veins.

G. ×*oxonianum* **'Katherine Adele'** ▲ 15 × 18 in. (38 × 45 cm). Heronswood Nursery, Washington, named and distributed this in 1997. It is a seedling selection from *G.* ×*oxonianum* 'Walter's Gift' with darker central bronzing of the leaf and silver-pink flowers veined in purple. It was originally suggested that it be grown in full sun, but in areas with high summer heat it needs afternoon shade.

G. ×*oxonianum* **'Königshof'** ◄ 30 × 30 in. (75 × 75 cm). Christian Kress of Sarastro Nursery, Austria, introduced this in 1996. It has large dark pink flowers with reddish-purple veins.

G. ×*oxonianum* **'Lace Time'** ▲ 15 × 15 in. (38 × 38 cm). Croftway Nursery, United Kingdom, introduced this in 1992. It is quite similar to one of its parents, *G. versicolor*, with white flowers and rose veins, but the flowers deepen to a pink color as the plant ages.

G. ×*oxonianum* **'Lady Moore'** 18 × 24 in. (45 × 60 cm). Reportedly Lady Moore of Dublin gave this to Margery Fish, United Kingdom. It has light green leaves with faint internodal blotches. The flowers are a dark luminous pink, becoming pale in the center, with purple veins. It has a long and heavy flowering from spring through summer.

G. ×*oxonianum* **'Laura Skelton'** ▲ 30 × 30 in. (75 × 75 cm). From Catforth Gardens, United Kingdom, and introduced by Judith Bradshaw in 2004. It has the tendency, like all the large-leaf forms of *G.* ×*oxonianum*, to grow its stems high out of the ground, so replant it every couple of years. It has remarkable flowers with a pale lavender background and numerous intricate purple veins.

G. ×*oxonianum* **'Lutzie'** ▼ 30 × 24 in. (75 × 60 cm). A seedling from *G.* ×*oxonianum* 'Claridge Druce'. Rainforest Gardens, British Columbia, Canada, introduced this in 1998. It has medium pink flowers with purple veins and a white throat and is a strong, vigorous plant.

G. ×*oxonianum* **'Maurice Moka'** 12 × 15 in. (30 × 38 cm). From Dirk de Winter, Netherlands. Similar to G. ×*oxonianum* 'Katherine Adele', but more compact. Leaves have a brown stain and flowers are light lavender-pink.

G. ×*oxonianum* **'Mistique'** ▼ 15 × 18 in. (38 × 45 cm). White flowers with light purple veins.

G. ×*oxonianum* **'Old Rose'** ▶ 15 × 18 in. (38 × 45 cm). Allan Robinson discovered and named this, and Axletree Nursery, United Kingdom, distributed it. A compact selection with medium green leaves and light red-pink flowers with dark veins. The color of the flower deepens with age to give the plant a multicolored effect.

G. ×*oxonianum* **'Pat Smallacombe'** 24 × 36 in. (60 × 90 cm). A chance seedling from the garden of Pat Smalla-combe, United Kingdom, which Judith Bradshaw of Cat-forth Gardens, United Kingdom, distributed in 1994. It has green large, deeply veined leaves with broadly toothed and deeply cut lobes. The large flowers are funnel shaped and deep pink with numerous deep red veins.

G. ×*oxonianum* **'Pearl Boland'** 18 × 24 in. (45 × 60 cm). A sterile hybrid from Terra Nova Nurseries, Oregon. The multicolored pink flowers darken as they age.

G. ×*oxonianum* **'Phoebe Noble'** ◀ 17 × 30 in. (43 × 75 cm). Found growing in the garden of Phoebe Noble; Elke and Ken Knechtel of Rainforest Gardens, British Columbia, Canada, named it after her in 1993. It has medium green, deeply veined, toothed leaves with deeply cut lobes. The flowers are strong dark pink with dark cherry veins. The flowers are the darkest of any in the G. ×*oxonianum* group.

G. ×*oxonianum* **'Phoebe's Blush'** 18 × 24 in. (45 × 60 cm). From Robin Moss, who named it after his mother. Catforth Gardens, United Kingdom, introduced it in 1995. The flowers age from light pink to dark pink, and there are no visible veins.

G. ×*oxonianum* **'Rebecca Moss'** ◀ 18 × 24 in. (45 × 60 cm). Robin Moss, United Kingdom, selected and named this in or prior to 1993. It has very pale pink flowers with grayish-green veins.

G. ×*oxonianum* **'Rose Clair'** 15 × 24 in. (38 × 60 cm). A. T. Johnson, Wales, raised this around 1940 and Ingwers-en's Nursery introduced it in 1946. It has rose-pink flow-ers that become deep pink with age. It is probably not the original introduction, which was described as "clear rose-salmon with a trace of veining."

G. ×*oxonianum* **'Rosenlicht'** 18 × 20 in. (45 × 50 cm). A selection from Heinz Klose, Germany. It has deep pink flow-ers with translucent veins. The selection is only slightly paler than G. ×*oxonianum* 'Phoebe Noble', and the two are diffi-cult to distinguish. The petals of 'Rosenlicht' appear to be slightly more rounded.

G. ×oxonianum 'Spring Fling' 14 × 24 in. (28 × 60 cm). This has variegated cream-and-green leaves, whose centers are green with pink internodal blotches. The leaves are irregularly sized. The flowers are narrowly petalled and pale pink with dark purple veins. New leaves are more prominently variegated and tend to turn yellow green in the summer.

G. ×oxonianum 'Summer Surprise' ▶ 18 × 30 in. (45 × 75 cm). From Piet Oudolf, Netherlands. It has large strong pink flowers and is in bloom for several months in cool summers.

G. ×oxonianum 'Susan' ▶ 15 × 18 in. (38 × 45 cm). Pale pink flowers with very strong purple veins. John Tuite, West Acre Gardens, Norfolk, United Kingdom, named this for his wife.

G. ×oxonianum f. thurstonianum ▼ 24 × 30 in. (60 × 75 cm). This appears to be one of the oldest of the G. ×oxonianum hybrids. A. E. Bowles first described it in 1914, in the United Kingdom, and it was first named in 1928. The flowers have twisted, narrow, notched deep-pink petals, fading paler to the center of the flower and with numerous magenta veins. The flowers are relatively small, 1¼ inches (3.1 cm), and the plant grows quite large, so site it carefully in the garden. The leaves are lightly blotched. The plant produces many seedlings, so it is impossible to know if we are still growing the original selection, but that is unlikely.

G. ×oxonianum f. thurstonianum 'Crûg Star' ◄ 18 × 24 in. (45 × 60 cm). Large bright pink open flowers with narrow starry petals that are strongly veined.

G. ×oxonianum f. thurstonianum 'Sherwood' 30 × 20 in. (75 × 50 cm). A garden seedling raised by D. Hibberd, Axletree Nursery, United Kingdom, and introduced in 1991. It has maroon internodal blotches on the leaves and a growth habit similar to *G.* ×oxonianum f. *thurstonianum*, but the flowers have very narrow pale pink petals. The flowers appear somewhat out of scale with the large coarse leaves, but the effect is interesting up close.

G. ×oxonianum f. thurstonianum 'Southcombe Double' ◄ 15 × 18 in. (38 × 45 cm). Southcombe Garden Plant Nursery, United Kingdom, introduced this in 1982. The medium green leaves have very faint internodal blotches. The flower has two phases. One-inch (2.5 cm) diameter single five-petalled flowers appear in the early spring, and five-petalled flowers with numerous petalloid stamens in midsummer. The flowers look like salmon-pink powder puffs. The plant is compact and not very vigorous, so place it where viewers can easily see the small flowers.

G. ×oxonianum 'Wageningen' 12 × 15 in. (30 × 38 cm). Of Dutch origin, selected by Hans Simon. It has warm salmon-pink flowers and compact growth that makes it very useful for the front of a perennial border or a container.

G. ×oxonianum 'Walter's Gift' ◀ 15 × 24 in. (38 × 60 cm). Appeared as a seedling in a garden named Walter's Gift, which belonged to Mary Ramsdale, United Kingdom. Cally Gardens introduced this in 1989. It has medium green shiny leaves with a maroon stain in the center and light pink flowers with dark lavender veins. It is possible to make selections from the seedlings of this plant to increase the size of the leaf zonation, as Heronswood Nursery, Washington, did with *G. ×oxonianum* 'Katherine Adele'.

G. ×oxonianum 'Wargrave Pink' ▲ (syn. *G. endressii* 'Wargrave Pink'). 17 × 20 in. (40 × 50 cm). Originally from Waterer, Son and Crisp Nursery, United Kingdom, in 1930. It is fairly certain that any plants sold in the United States are seedlings of 'Wargrave Pink'. Nurseries produce a wide range of plants known as 'Wargrave Pink', some of which have dark-veined petals and flowers of varying shades of pink. It is widely distributed in the United States and is sometimes seen as a survival plant in old, abandoned gardens. The leaves are medium green with five lobes, and the flowers are medium pink with a faint blue cast and notched petals. In mild climates it will flower sporadically from spring through fall and ultimately form a spreading ground cover.

G. ×oxonianum 'Winscombe' 15 × 20 in. (38 × 50 cm). Margery Fish discovered this in a garden in the United Kingdom. It forms medium green mounds of multicolored flowers that open to pale pink and change to deep pink as they age. It has light purple veins. It is a compact and highly useful plant for the front of a border that receives morning sun, and as an underpinning for light shade shrubs.

SHADE

Almost all shade-loving geraniums will tolerate some early morning summer sun and light shade after midmorning. Areas that receive no sunlight at all pose a problem. These are locations shaded by perennial trees and shrubs with heavy leaf cover, or structures such as walls and fences. If you cannot introduce light by pruning, select some shade-tolerant plants other than hardy geraniums. Most shade geraniums will do well in light and dappled shade. But as the seasons change, areas that were light in spring become darker as perennial shrubs gain heavier leaf cover. If the plants decline substantially in vigor, you may need to move them.

Geraniums generally should be watered during the summer, but some of the eastern Mediterranean geraniums will survive during the summer with just occasional water. Drainage is more important, as shade geraniums respond well to good drainage. Unless noted, most prefer soil that is watered, allowed to go partially dry, and then watered again, rather than soil that is kept uniformly moist.

Geranium cataractarum

A small mounding plant with distinctive five-lobed dissected ferny leaves that are aromatic and deeply divided. It has rose-pink flowers with orange anthers that are slightly less than ¾ inch (1.9 cm) wide.

ZONES 7–9
PLANT SIZE 8 × 12 in. (20 × 30 cm)
SOIL Well-drained loam amended with concrete chips; oyster grit to increase alkalinity if necessary
LIGHT Shade
PROPAGATION Seed
ORIGIN Native to southeastern Spain and Morocco. Found on damp and shady limestone rocks. *G. cataractarum* and its subspecies both flower in late spring and early summer.
GARDEN AND DESIGN USES Fern garden, trough, or dish garden
NOTES Do not allow it to dry out.
SUBSPECIES
G. cataractarum **subsp.** *pitardii* A subspecies from Morocco that has rounded leaf lobes and flowers that are paler pink than *G. cataractarum*.

Geranium gracile

The pale green leaves are large, five- to seven-lobed, and hairy. The plant has a thick branched rootstock and a mounding habit. The flowering stems are tall, and the flowers are funnel shaped, medium pink becoming greenish in the center, with notched petals. Short purple veins give the best forms of these flowers an attractive eyelash appearance, but there are many forms circulating in nurseries in which the strong veins are absent.

ZONES 5–9
PLANT SIZE 30–36 × 30 in. (75–90 × 75 cm)

SOIL Moderately moist, well-drained loam, slightly acidic to neutral
LIGHT Morning sun and afternoon shade
PROPAGATION Seed for species, crown division for cultivars
ORIGIN From northeastern Turkey, southern Caucasus, and northern Iran
GARDEN AND DESIGN USES Shade garden, back of a shade border, shrub border in light shade
NOTES Does well where it receives plentiful summer water and protection from strong sun, which tends to yellow the leaves.

CULTIVARS

***G. gracile* 'Blanche'** ▲ 24–30 × 30 in. (60–75 × 75 cm). Axletree Nursery distributed this in 1994. The plant has beautiful funnel-shaped flowers that are white with lavender on the outer edges of the notched petals. The prominent eyelash veins are purple. As is the case with the species, the flowers are a little too small to be in balance with the large leaves. It is a useful background plant for a shady area where a large mound of leaves is needed for an accent.

***G. gracile* 'Blush'** ▶ 30–36 × 30 in. (75–90 × 75 cm). From the United Kingdom in 1993. It has strong pink funnel-shaped flowers with notched petals and short purple veins.

HYBRIDS

***G.* 'Chantilly'** Parentage *G. gracile* × *G. renardii*. 15 × 18 in. (38 × 45 cm). Hybridized by Alan Bremner, introduced by Axletree Nursery, United Kingdom, in 1991. Form somewhat similar to *G. gracile* with large, leafy clumps and light lavender-pink flowers. Relatively well behaved. Appears to be sterile.

Geranium maderense

A large, cold-sensitive (less than 28°F [–2°C]) biennial rosette plant. It forms a mound of large dinner plate–size leaves at the end of fleshy red-brown leaf stems. As the plant matures, these stems bend over and serve as a prop for the main stem, which grows upward over an approximately two-year period, accelerating as flowering approaches. The many flowers are displayed on a very large head and are rounded, slightly convex, and deep pink illuminated by numerous pale and elevated veins. Brilliant purple hairs trap insects on the flowering stems.

ZONES 8–10, cold sensitive below 28°F (–2°C)
PLANT SIZE 48–60 × 36–48 in. (122–152 × 90–122 cm)
SOIL Well-drained loam, slightly acidic to neutral
LIGHT Morning sun in mild summer gardens to light shade in hot summer gardens
PROPAGATION Seed
ORIGIN The species is found on the island of Madeira in the North Atlantic off the coast of North Africa, although it is thought to have been introduced and to have settled itself in South Africa, California, and the Channel Islands of the United Kingdom. It has also hybridized with *G. reuteri*, *G. palmatum*, and *G. yeoi*.

GARDEN AND DESIGN USES This is a desirable plant for mild winter gardens. It grows during winter and flowers in spring. It is the second-largest geranium, and the huge bouquet of flowers that usually appears in the spring of the second to third year makes a dramatic display, so provide enough space to accommodate this. It looks handsome among spring-flowering shrubs and trees. Unfortunately, deer find the leaves extremely palatable.

NOTES No one knows what triggers the flowering of this plant, although it may be increasing day length, intensity of light, a change in air temperature, or rising soil temperatures. However, flowering can take as long as two to five years. Not all plants in any particular area will flower at the same time. It seeds profusely, but the seedlings are easy to remove. It does not grow to its full potential in a container, although in cold areas it is possible to grow it in a large container in a conservatory or greenhouse (flower heads will still be smaller). Small containers produce cramped plants. It dies after flowering, although occasionally offsets form around the base.

Note that *G. maderense* is on the IUCN Red List of Threatened Species because of habitat destruction and invasive species in its native Madeira.

CULTIVARS

G. maderense 'Guernsey White' ▼ 36–40 × 36 in. (90–102 × 90 cm). Ray Brown, United Kingdom, raised this. Flowers are white with a pink center and leaf stems are green. Isolate plants from *G. maderense* to maintain the white flowers. Some seed selections with all white flowers and no pink center have been made, notably by Ron Vanderhoff, nursery manager of Rogers Gardens, Corona del Mar, California.

Geranium ×monacense

Forms a mound of leaves that may show prominent blotches, with flowers held well above the leaves. The small flowers are purple-red or pink-lilac, with a blue-lilac zone above a whitish petal base. The petals are strongly reflexed.

ZONES 4–10
PLANT SIZE 18–24 × 18 in. (45–60 × 45 cm)
SOIL Loam, slightly acidic to neutral
LIGHT Morning sun and afternoon shade in mild summer gardens, light shade in hot summer gardens
ORIGIN *G. phaeum* × *G. reflexum*. Dr. K. Harz found the plant in his garden in Upper Bavaria and named it after the city of Munich. There are different selections in cultivation, some of which A. E. Bowles described in 1914.
GARDEN AND DESIGN USES Shade gardens and shrub borders, containers for light shade
PROPAGATION Crown division

NOTES Very easy to grow and a sweet selection for the shade. The flowers are small, so site the plants where viewers can see them easily.

VARIETIES

G. ×*monacense* var. *anglicum* ▲ 18–24 × 24 in. (45–60 × 60 cm). Flowers are pink-lilac with a white petal base that has a blue-violet zone above it. The plant is quite vigorous.

CULTIVARS

G. ×*monacense* 'Breckland Fever' 15 × 18 in. (38 × 45 cm). The Plantsman's Preference Nursery, United Kingdom, selected this in 2002 and described it as having "deliriously feverish rosy mauve flowers. It's also extremely spotty."

G. ×*monacense* 'Claudine Dupont' ◄ 18 × 18 in. (45 × 45 cm). Claudine Dupont selected this and Y. Gosse de Gorre, France, introduced it in 1996. It has "reflexed dusky-pink petals with a grayish-blue ring that changes to blue at the base of the petals." The leaves have brown blotches.

G. ×*monacense* 'Mrs. Charles Perrin' 18 × 24 in. (45 × 60 cm). From the Margery Fish Nursery, United Kingdom, in 1993. A selection made at East Lambrook Manor. The flowers are a light mauve with a blue ring, becoming paler toward the center of the flower. The edges are slightly ruffled.

G. ×*monacense* 'Muldoon' 18–24 × 18 in. (45–60 × 45 cm). Richard Clifton named it in 1979 after the character Spotty Muldoon on the United Kingdom radio show *The Goon Show*. It has prominent brown internodal leaf blotches. Its flowers are reflexed and lilac-purple with a white base.

Geranium nodosum

Spreads by underground rhizomatous roots and forms medium-size mounds of dark green shiny, deeply veined, three- to five-lobed and toothed leaves. The funnel-shaped flowers range in color from lavender to dark pink to almost maroon, and grow 1 inch (2.5 cm) wide. The petals are notched and wedge shaped.

ZONES 5–9
PLANT SIZE 10 × 20 in. (25 × 50 cm)
SOIL Well-drained moderately moist loam, slightly acidic to neutral
LIGHT Light to medium shade
PROPAGATION Seed (for species), crown division, roots
ORIGIN Central France to Pyrenees, central Italy, central Balkans. Found in mountain forests.
GARDEN AND DESIGN USES Shade garden, shrub garden
NOTES At least two sources have reported that G. nodosum can become invasive and that it is very difficult to eradicate. The roots break into small segments that will grow and produce new plants.
CULTIVARS
G. nodosum **'Clos du Coudray'** ▶ 10 × 20 in. (25 × 50 cm). Flowers with rosy purple petals, purple veins, and white edges. Named after a garden in the north of France.
G. nodosum **'Jenny'** 15 × 20 in. (38 × 50 cm). A larger, more vigorous form of G. 'Svelte Lilac' with pale lavender flowers.

G. nodosum 'Silverwood' ▶ 10–12 × 20 in. (25–30 × 50 cm). Small white flowers with notched petals and green veins. Joan Taylor introduced this for the Motor Neurone Disease Association in memory of her late husband and described it in the Birchwood catalog, United Kingdom, in 2003.

G. nodosum 'Svelte Lilac' ▶ 12 × 20 in. (30 × 50 cm). From Monksilver Nursery, United Kingdom, in 1990. It is a distinctive and choice selection, growing mounds of light green leaves and pale lilac flowers with dark veins and a white eye. It remains more compact and slightly taller than the species.

G. nodosum 'Swish Purple' 10 × 15 in. (25 × 38 cm). From Monksilver Nursery, United Kingdom, in 1990. It is a very dark purple-flowered selection, with petals fading paler to the center and red veins.

G. nodosum 'Tony's Talisman' 12 × 20 in. (30 × 50 cm). Flowers are brilliant magenta with an even darker magenta blotch at the base of the notched petals, and a small white center.

G. nodosum 'Whiteleaf' ▶ 12 × 20 in. (30 × 50 cm). Found in the Maritime Alps. Lionel Bacon, United Kingdom, selected this and named it after his garden. Monksilver Nursery, United Kingdom, first offered it in 1992. It is distinguished by its very unusual flowers, which are lavender with magenta blotches and a pale edge around the petals. They are highly visible in medium shade.

Geranium palmatum

An open, spreading mound with long flowering stems. It forms a large rosette with deeply divided palmate leaves that can be more than 12 inches (30 cm) wide. Flowering stems arise from the base and form a tall, airy inflorescence with many medium pink flowers with red-pink centers.

ZONES 8–10; cold sensitive below 28°F (−2°C); damage and death may occur fairly rapidly at lower temperatures

PLANT SIZE 36–48 × 36–48 in. (90–122 × 90–122 cm)

SOIL Well-drained, neutral to slightly acidic

LIGHT Morning sun in mild summer gardens to light shade in hot summer gardens

PROPAGATION Seed

ORIGIN Found on the island of Madeira and cultivated in Europe for more than 200 years.

GARDEN AND DESIGN USES Mild-climate gardens in morning sun to light shade borders or among deciduous trees and shrubs. It looks spectacular against a colored wall.

NOTES The plant is short lived, usually for one or at the most two seasons. It seeds freely, but the unwanted seedlings are easy to remove. *Geranium palmatum, G. maderense, G. yeoi,* and *G. robertianum* all hybridize among themselves in gardens, so take care to isolate each species if you plan successive crops of a particular species. There are no named hybrids.

    Geranium palmatum is sometimes confused with *G. maderense.* However, the plant structure is quite different. Leaves and flowering stems on *G. palmatum* arise from a fist-size crown or condensed stem at ground level, whereas *G. maderense* has a thick tall central stem that appears when the plant is getting ready to flower.

    Transplant *G. palmatum* seedlings when young. Older plants do not tolerate the transplanting process well.

Geranium phaeum

A remarkably tough and hardy spring-flowering plant. After flowering it forms a large ground-level mound for the remainder of the season. The dark green leaves are broadly divided into seven segments that are prominently toothed. Some leaves are all dark green or blotched dark brown, usually at the internodes; variegated in cream, yellow, and pink; or all yellow. Flowers are the size and shape of a dime, nodding, slightly reflexed, and ¾ inch (1.9 cm) in diameter. There are two forms, as well as a very large number of cultivars. In *G. phaeum* var. *phaeum*, the flowers are colored purple or maroon, and in *G. phaeum* var. *lividum* they are white, lavender, or pink with a white base that is often preceded by a bluish ring.

ZONES 4–9

PLANT SIZE 12–36 × 18–36 in. (30–90 × 45–90 cm)

SOIL Light to medium loam, slightly acidic to neutral. In nature it sometimes grows in damp meadows, but it can withstand some dryness as well. It is also found in disturbed ground.

LIGHT Light shade

ORIGIN Found in mountainous areas in south and central Europe from the Pyrenees through the Alps, to Croatia, Ukraine, Romania, and Bulgaria.

PROPAGATION Seed for species, crown division for named cultivars

GARDEN AND DESIGN USES Indispensable for shade gardens. Tolerates lesser to greater amounts of shade and can be useful in shrub borders and alongside houses where fences or other houses block strong light.

NOTES If plants look untidy after they have finished flowering in the spring, you can shear them back to the crown and they will regrow leaves, although usually not flower again, unless the weather is very mild. Shearing has the added advantage of preventing masses of seedlings. There are more than 75 named forms of *G. phaeum*, so concentrate on your top picks.

CULTIVARS

G. phaeum 'Advendo' ◀ 18 × 24 in. (45 × 60 cm). The flowers are purple-red and have a bluish ring next to their white base.

***G. phaeum* 'Album'** ▶ 24 × 36 in. (60 × 90 cm). A white-flowered form of *G. phaeum* var. *phaeum* from 1940, originally wild collected in Switzerland and published as *G. phaeum* var. *album*.

***G. phaeum* 'Calligrapher'** ◀ 18 × 24 in. (45 × 60 cm). John Sirkett of Mallorn Gardens, United Kingdom, raised this, and Axletree Nursery, United Kingdom, published it in 1993. The flowers are a washed-out pale lavender with slightly darker edges at the top of the petals. There are dark purple-feathered edges to the white zone near the base. The petals are frilled and slightly pointed at the top and the foliage is prominently blotched with brown.

***G. phaeum* 'Chocolate Chip'** ▼ 18 × 24 in. (45 × 60 cm). Geraniaceae Nursery, California, selected this in 1995. Flowers are the color of dark chocolate. Leaves are unblotched.

G. phaeum 'Golden Spring' 20 × 30 in. (50 × 75 cm). From Catforth Gardens, United Kingdom. Robin Moss and Judith Bradshaw collected this in Scottish gardens. It has red-brown flowers and leaves that are yellow in the spring and green in the summer.

G. phaeum 'Lady in Mourning' 12 × 15 in. (30 × 38 cm). David Victor, Geranium Registrar, chose this name in 2008 to replace 'Mourning Widow'. The flowers are dark brown, the flowering stems are red brown, and the leaves are unblotched.

G. phaeum 'Langthorn's Blue' 18 × 24 in. (45 × 60 cm). Langthorn's Plantery, United Kingdom, introduced this in 1987. The flowers are slightly bluer than G. phaeum 'Calligrapher', and the leaves are unblotched.

G. phaeum 'Lily Lovell' ◀ 15–18 × 24 in. (38–45 × 60 cm). Trevor Bath, United Kingdom, raised this and named it after his mother. The flowers are dark violet-blue.

G. phaeum 'Little Boy' 10 × 12 in. (25 × 30 cm). J. Boterdael found this in Belgium in a friend's garden. The leaves are all green and the flowers are purple-brown.

G. phaeum var. lividum 'Alec's Pink' 18 × 24 in. (45 × 60 cm). Alec Anderson found the seedling and LW Plants, United Kingdom, named it for him in 2000. It has medium blue-pink flowers.

G. phaeum var. lividum 'All Saints' ◀ 18 × 24 in. (45 × 60 cm). From Monksilver Nursery, United Kingdom, in 1996. The flowers are very pale pink-violet with a gray overlay.

G. phaeum var. lividum 'Blue Shadow' 18–24 × 18–24 in. (45–60 × 45–60 cm). From The Plantsman's Preference Nursery, United Kingdom, in 1998. Its pale lavender flowers are said to have a blue appearance, especially in shade. The flowers have a dark central ring.

G. phaeum var. lividum 'Joan Baker' 18–24 × 24 in. (45–60 × 60 cm). A. W. A. (Bill) Baker raised this seedling from a plant he collected and named after his wife. From Axletree Nursery, United Kingdom, in 1991. It has large light pink flowers.

G. phaeum var. lividum 'Lavender Pinwheel'
18 × 24 in. (45 × 60 cm). De Vrooman, Inc. selected this
from a garden in the Netherlands. Leaves are blotched
maroon-brown in the internodes. The flowers appear
painted in watercolor. They have light purple bleeding from
a thin purple line near the base of the petals, a pale lavender center, and a purple edge to the petals.

G. phaeum var. lividum 'Majus' ▲ 24 × 36 in. (60 × 90
cm). Peter Yeo used this name in 1985 to correct the name
'Major' following *The Cultivated Plant Code*. Flowers are
lilac with a purple tone.

G. phaeum var. lividum 'Merry Widow' ▶ 12 × 18 in.
(30 × 45 cm). From Geraniaceae Nursery, California, in
2010. Its large flowers have slightly ruffled petals of the
palest lilac. They have a blue-purple ring near the base, and
purple veins bleeding into the pale petals.

G. phaeum var. lividum 'Mierhausen' 20 × 30 in. (50 ×
75 cm). From Germany. Light lavender flowers with slightly
darker edges and a light violet ring near the base.

G. phaeum var. lividum 'Rose Air' 18 × 20 in. (45 × 50
cm). J. Sirkett, Mallorn Gardens, Cornwall, United Kingdom, raised this. It has medium green unblotched leaves
and flowers of the palest possible lilac pink, almost white.
However, it was originally described as having red-purple
flowers, so there has clearly been some confusion.

G. phaeum var. **lividum** **'Rose Madder'** ◄ 18 × 24 in. (45 × 60 cm). Trevor Bath, United Kingdom, introduced this around 1986. The flower color is a very unusual brown-pink and the leaves have small brown internodal blotches.

G. phaeum var. **lividum** **'Stillingfleet Ghost'** 18 × 24 in. (45 × 60 cm). Vanessa Cook of Stillingfleet Nursery, United Kingdom, introduced this around 1986. It has moonbeam gray flowers and unblotched green leaves.

G. phaeum var. **lividum** **'Walküre'** 20 × 24 in. (50 × 60 cm). From Sarastro Nursery, Austria, in 1999, and raised by Christian Kress. Leaves are light green without markings. The flowers are palest lavender with a light blue-gray ring near the base, a pale center, and stronger lavender on the edges of the petals. They are slightly larger than average.

G. phaeum **'Margaret Wilson'** 12 × 18 in. (30 × 45 cm). Axletree Nursery, United Kingdom, introduced this in 1989. It has reticulated yellow and very light green leaves, and blue-lavender flowers with a white eye. Grow this in the shade, as it will burn in the sun.

G. phaeum **'Mierhausen'** 20 × 30 in. (50 × 75 cm). Light lavender flowers with slightly darker edges and a light violet ring near the base of the flowers.

G. phaeum **'Mrs. Withey-Price'** ▼ 15 × 18 in. (38 × 45 cm). Brilliant yellow leaves with red intermodal blotches emerge in the spring, later becoming medium green. The flowers are lavender-pink with a mauve ring and a white center.

G. phaeum 'Our Pat' 24 × 36 in. (60 × 90 cm). Marie Addeyman found this and named it in her sister's garden. It has very dark chocolate-purple flowers with a small white base.

G. phaeum 'Rachel's Rhapsody' 18 × 24 in. (45 × 60 cm). Rachel Etheridge found the seedling, and The Plantsman's Preference distributed it in 2003. The leaves are dark green and irregularly splashed with yellow. The flowers are purple.

G. phaeum 'Raven' 18 × 24 in. (45 × 60 cm). A seedling of *G. phaeum* 'Lily Lovell'. Rainforest Gardens, Canada, introduced this in 1998. It has deep purple flowers and brown-blotched leaves. However, the blotching trait seems to have disappeared from plants currently available in nurseries.

G. phaeum 'Samobor' ◀ 15 × 20 in. (38 × 50 cm). Maroon flowers and leaves that have a broad band of brown in the center of the leaf. It has been produced by seed commercially, and the brown zone is sometimes quite small. Look for selections with good, broad zonation.

G. phaeum 'Séricourt' 15 × 18 in. (38 × 45 cm). Bob Brown of Cotswold Garden Flowers, United Kingdom, found this in the French village of Séricourt. It has beautiful new yellow leaves in early spring and red-brown flowers. The leaves change to yellow-green in the summer.

G. phaeum 'Shadowlight' 15 × 18 in. (38 × 45 cm). The leaves have a light cream center, brown internodal blotches, and streaks and splashes of cream extending through the lobes. Flowers are maroon-purple.

G. phaeum 'Springtime' 18 × 24 in. (45 × 60 cm). Nurseryman and garden designer Piet Oudolf found this in the Netherlands in 1999. The leaves are well marked with cream, light green, and red toward their centers, and change to deeper green-yellow in midsummer. The flowers are red-brown. Restricted to licensed propagators.

G. phaeum **'Taff's Jester'** 15 × 18 in. (38 × 45 cm). Stephen Taffler, United Kingdom, found this, and Axletree Nursery published it in 1989. The leaves are irregularly splashed with cream and the flowers are red-brown.

G. phaeum **'Tricia'** ▼ 18 × 24 in. (45 × 60 cm). Selected by Geraniaceae Nursery, California. Very dark chocolate-purple colored flowers. The leaves are unblotched.

G. phaeum **'Variegatum'** 14 × 18 in. (36 × 45 cm). The variegated leaves have blotches of cream, yellow, white, and a little red. Leaves tend to become green in the summer, and you can cut back the whole plant to promote new variegated leaves. The flowers are red-brown.

HYBRIDS

G. ×*monacense*

Geranium pyrenaicum

Can form very large mounds in gardens. It has attractive medium green leaves that are wide and rounded with seven to nine shallow divisions and masses of small ½-inch (1.25 cm) starry flowers with notched petals that appear in white, pink, or purple on long flowering stems.

ZONES 7–9
PLANT SIZE 15 × 24 in. (38 × 60 cm)
SOIL Well-drained loam to fast-draining gravel soils, alkaline to neutral to slightly acidic
LIGHT Full sun to half shade

PROPAGATION Seed
ORIGIN It is widespread in southwestern and Eastern Europe, and naturalized in the United Kingdom. It grows on the edges of woods, in scrub, in meadows, and in ground that has been disturbed.
GARDEN AND DESIGN USES Perennial borders, containers, gravel gardens, rock gardens
NOTES Seedlings are easy to pull up. The plant is short lived.
FORMS
G. pyrenaicum* f. *albiflorum ◄ 18 × 24 in. (45 × 60 cm). A. W. A. (Bill) Baker collected this form in Switzerland and introduced it. The plant has the same medium green gently rounded leaves and small white scalloped flowers that bloom profusely throughout the growing season. It can bloom itself out, and you can cut it back to produce new flowering stems. Because it seeds readily, you can select new seedlings for the following year. There is another white-flowered form of *G. pyrenaicum* available, 'Summer Snow', which has slightly larger flowers.
CULTIVARS
***G. pyrenaicum* 'Bill Wallis'** ◄ 18 × 24 in. (45 × 60 cm). Named after Bill Wallis of The Useful Plant Company in Cambridgeshire, United Kingdom. This is a fine selection with medium green leaves and small vivid purple flowers in great profusion over a long flowering period. It appears to flower true from seed as long as it is isolated from the other color forms of *G. pyrenaicum*.
***G. pyrenaicum* 'Isparta'** 20 × 24 in. (50 × 60 cm). Named by Peter Yeo, who collected the cultivar in Turkey in 1989. The flowers and leaves are larger than the species and the flowers are blue-pink with a small white center.

Geranium rectum

Clump-forming, glossy green leaves that are sharply toothed and five to seven lobed. It has bright rose-pink vase-shaped flowers with notched petals. Flowers are 1 inch (2.5 cm).

ZONES 5–9
PLANT SIZE 20 × 20 in. (50 × 50 cm)
SOIL Well-drained loam, slightly acidic to neutral
LIGHT Light and bright shade
PROPAGATION Roots, seed
ORIGIN Kashmir, Kazakhstan, Kyrgyzstan, Pakistan, and Tian Shan, China. It grows between 4500 and 7800 feet (1370–2370 m) in forest meadows.
GARDEN AND DESIGN USES Woodlands, shrub borders in light shade
NOTES This plant is not of great horticultural interest, being more for collectors, but some gardeners like to use it in their gardens, possibly because of the name.

Geranium reflexum ▸

Makes a mound with five to seven broadly lobed leaves that have small maroon internodal blotches. The plant has tall flowering stems with flowers that are deeply reflexed and quite small. The species has rose-pink flowers with a blue zone above a white base. There is some variation in color and one named selection.

ZONES 4–10
PLANT SIZE 18 × 20 in. (45 × 50 cm)
SOIL Moderately moist loam with good drainage, neutral to slightly alkaline
LIGHT Light shade
PROPAGATION Crown division, seed
ORIGIN Found in mountain woods and meadows in Europe, including central Italy and the Balkans.
GARDEN AND DESIGN USES Shade garden
NOTES Place G. reflexum in the shade garden where viewers can see the flowers up close.
CULTIVARS
G. reflexum 'Katara Pass' ▸ 24 × 24 in. (60 × 60 cm). Lionel Bacon collected this in the Katara Pass in the Pindus Mountains, Greece. It was described in 2008 in *Register of Geranium Cultivar Names* as having "dingy dark violet flowers and unspotted leaves."
HYBRIDS
G. ×monacense

Geranium reuteri

SYNONYM *G. canariense*

An annual to a short-lived perennial. It forms a large rosette of green slightly shiny palmate leaves that have five deep and pinnate lobes. The plant produces inflorescences that are up to 36 inches (90 cm) tall, very branched, and covered with magenta glandular hairs on the upper stems. The stems and leaves feel somewhat succulent. The 1 ¼-inch (3.1 cm) diameter flowers are deep pink with a white center and separated petals.

ZONES 9–10
PLANT SIZE 36 × 36–40 in. (90 × 90–102 cm)
SOIL Medium loam, well-drained, slightly acidic to neutral to slightly alkaline
LIGHT Morning sun and afternoon shade in cool summer gardens, light shade in hot summer gardens
PROPAGATION Seed
ORIGIN Found on the Canary Islands. Grows in shady locations along with trees and shrubs.
GARDEN AND DESIGN USES A large imposing plant for light shade locations in a shade border.
NOTES Seeds prolifically, but the seedlings are easy to pull up. It has been known as *G. canariense*, but Carlos Aedo and Félix Munoz suggested a new name because *canariense* was originally proposed for a pelargonium. However, it is found in the literature mostly under its old name. Plant this only in milder areas along the Pacific Coast, as it grows in winter and flowers in spring. It is not winter hardy below around 28°F (–2°C), but you could grow it in a temperature-controlled greenhouse.

HYBRIDS Fertile hybrids with *G. yeoi*, *G. palmatum*, and *G. robertianum* have been noted, but are unnamed. It is important to keep stock of *G. reuteri* separate from other members of this group—*G. maderense, G. palmatum, G. robertianum* and *G. yeoi*—as they will hybridize. The hybrids are generally not as attractive as the parents.

Geranium shikokianum ▲

A bushy plant with leaves that are marbled above, shiny beneath, and divided into five to seven deep and broad lobes. The rootstock is fleshy. Funnel-shaped flowers are 1¼ inches (3.1 cm) wide and pink with a white center and light purple netted veins.

ZONES 7–9, possibly lower
PLANT SIZE 15 × 24 in. (38 × 60 cm)
SOIL Well-drained loam, slightly acidic to neutral
LIGHT Light shade
PROPAGATION Seed, roots (the roots break apart easily)
ORIGIN Japan and Korea
GARDEN AND DESIGN USES Ground cover for light shade
NOTES Collectors have gathered a number of different varieties of this species, and some are more compact than others. It is very easy to propagate from the roots.
VARIETIES
G. shikokianum var. *kaimontanum* 12 × 15 in. (30 × 38 cm). The leaves are rounded, shallowly lobed, and lightly marbled with reddish stems. Flowers are deep pink with a small white center and purple veins.
G. shikokianum var. *quelpartense* 10 × 15 in. (25 × 38 cm). A small, low-growing plant from Quelpart Island, between Japan and Korea. It has densely hairy leaves, and pink-and-white flowers.
G. shikokianum var. *shikokianum* 15 × 18 in. (38 × 45 cm). From mainland Japan. It has marbled leaves and open growth, and is less hairy than the species.
G. shikokianum var. *yoshiianum* 6 × 12 in. (15 × 30 cm). A dwarf form from Yakushima, Japan. It has marbled leaves and pale pink flowers with green-white centers and purple veins.

Geranium sylvaticum

A moderately large mound with deeply divided, seven- to nine-lobed leaves whose divisions are copiously toothed. Flowers vary from purple-violet to pink to white, and are 1¼ inches (3.1 cm) wide.

ZONES 5–9, possibly lower
PLANT SIZE 24 × 30 in. (60 × 75 cm)
SOIL Moderately damp, well-drained loam, slightly acidic to neutral to alkaline
LIGHT Light shade
PROPAGATION Crown division and seed for species, forms, and varieties; crown division for cultivars and hybrids
ORIGIN Found in meadows in the mountains of southern Europe, down to sea level further north to the Arctic Circle, and is also native to the United Kingdom, where it appears along roadsides and streams and in lightly shaded areas.
GARDEN AND DESIGN USES In shade gardens and shrub borders, under fruit and nut trees
NOTES There are many selected color forms. This is a classic meadow and woodland plant requiring light shade and summer water. You can shear it to the ground in midseason to promote new leaves, but normally it will produce no additional flowers until the following spring.

VARIETIES

G. sylvaticum var. *wanneri* 18 × 18 in. (45 × 45 cm). Similar to *G. sylvaticum* 'Angulatum', but the flowers are smaller and rose pink with rose veins. According to Peter Yeo, it was collected in the Genevan Alps.

FORMS

G. sylvaticum f. *albiflorum* 24 × 18 in. (60 × 45 cm). A white variant of *G. sylvaticum* that retains its pink color on the sepals, stamens, and stigmas. It is found in the wild.

CULTIVARS

G. sylvaticum 'Album' ◀ 20 × 24 in. (50 × 60 cm). A bushy mound of soft pale green deeply lobed leaves and cupped white flowers with separated petals. It is totally anthocyanin free, and thus pure green and white with no additional colors. It comes true from seed.
G. sylvaticum 'Amy Doncaster' ▲ 20 × 24 in. (50 × 60 cm). This appeared in the garden of Amy Doncaster, and Washfield Nursery, United Kingdom, distributed it in 1989. It has deep blue flowers with a white center.

G. sylvaticum 'Angulatum' 24–30 × 24 in. (60–75 × 60 cm). According to *Register of Geranium Cultivar Names*, this first appeared in *Curtis's Botanical Magazine* in 1792, and was later known as *G. sylvaticum* var. *angulatum*. It has light pink flowers with darker veins. The petals are large, broad, and notched. *Angulatum* refers to the stems, but it is rather difficult to tell.

G. sylvaticum 'Baker's Pink' 36–40 × 24 in. (90–102 × 60 cm). A. W. A. (Bill) Baker collected this near Wengen in the Swiss Alps, and Corsley Mill Nursery, United Kingdom, introduced it in 1988. This is a tall growing form with attractive pale pink flowers. It has a long flowering period, producing flowering stems from spring until fall, if the weather remains cool. Place it in the middle to the back of a shade border.

G. sylvaticum 'Birch Lilac' 24 × 20 in. (60 × 50 cm). Elke and Ken Knechtel of Rainforest Gardens in British Columbia, Canada, introduced this in 1997. It has lilac-colored flowers.

G. sylvaticum 'Immaculée' 20 × 24 in. (50 × 60 cm). From Coen Jansen at Vaste Planten, Netherlands, in 1992. The plant makes a large mound and has large white flowers with clear veins. It is very effective as an underplanting for trees and shrubs, and makes an excellent ground cover. It sometimes flowers twice in the same season.

G. sylvaticum 'Kanzlersgrund' 40 × 30 in. (102 × 75 cm). Tall growing with purple flowers.

G. sylvaticum 'Mayflower' ▲ 20 × 24 in. (50 × 60 cm). Alan Bloom of Bressingham Gardens raised the plant and introduced it in 1973. It has blue-lilac flowers with a small white eye. You can use it to great effect as a ground cover in filtered light to light shade locations.

G. sylvaticum 'Meran' 24–30 × 24 in. (60–75 × 60 cm). Heinz Klose, Germany, found this in Italy in 1968, named it for the northern Italian town of Merano, and introduced it in 1972. The flowers are dark purple.

G. sylvaticum 'Nikita' ◀ 24 × 24 in. (60 × 60 cm). A chance seedling from Heronswood Nursery, Washington, in 1998, and named after Dan Hinkley's pet spaniel. The flowers are medium lavender-blue with a white eye.

G. sylvaticum 'Silva' 20 × 24 in. (50 × 60 cm). From Ernst Pagels Nursery, Germany, in 1980. This form was collected in the wild. The flowers are violet.

Geranium versicolor

A mound of green hairy leaves that are broadly pointed with five lobes. The leaves often have brown blotches. The flowers are 1¼ inches (3.1 cm) wide, erect, and vase shaped with notched lobes. They have a white background that is intricately veined in purple.

ZONES 5–10
PLANT SIZE 18 × 24 in. (45 × 60 cm)
SOIL All types of soils, but flourishes in moderately damp loam, slightly acidic to neutral
LIGHT Light shade
PROPAGATION Crown division, seed
ORIGIN Central and southern Italy, Sicily, and the southern part of the Balkan Peninsula, which includes Greece and Albania. It grows in open woods, scrub, and grasslands.
GARDEN AND DESIGN USES Woodland garden, wild garden
NOTES Usually retains its leaves during the winter. The plant seeds vigorously, so take care not to introduce it into areas where you cannot easily remove it. It has been introduced into the wild in Virginia and West Virginia, which could become a problem.
CULTIVARS
***G. versicolor* 'Snow White'** (syn. *G. versicolor* 'White Lady') The name was first published in the Axletree Catalog, United Kingdom, in 1993. It has white flowers with colorless veins.

SCRAMBLERS AND CRAWLERS

Perennial scramblers and crawlers produce long flowering stems from a central rosette of leaves. In the course of a single growing season, these trailing stems can cover very wide areas. If they become too long, you can remove them at the end of the growing season and the plant will revert to the normal size of the basal mound. You can also prune back the stems and leaves in midseason for a renewal of basal leaves and, in some cases, new flowering stems.

Long trailing stems might seem like an invitation to disaster. Some geraniums in this section have stem leaves that are small or absent, and the stems are most attractive when they droop their way around and across other perennials and shrubs, producing, over a long growing season, their scattered but brightly colored flowers. In hot climates these stems can be leafless and are best hidden. Other widely spreading scramblers provide a low carpet-like cover that smothers weeds.

Geranium albanum ▶

Forms a basal clump of broadly lobed and rounded leaves with trailing flowering stems. The medium green leaves are rounded and toothed, and have seven to nine lobes. Flowers are bright pink with light magenta veins.

ZONES 5–9
PLANT SIZE 15 × 24 in. (38 × 60 cm)
SOIL Well-drained, dryish, slightly acidic to neutral to slightly alkaline
LIGHT Morning sun and afternoon shade; grow it in partial shade, as the leaves burn in hot, sunny gardens
PROPAGATION Crown division, seed
ORIGIN Found in nature in the southeast Caucasus and nearby Iran, mainly under shrubs.
GARDEN AND DESIGN USES Useful for the wild garden. You can used it to good effect growing through another geranium, such as G. *himalayense*, where the two flowers combine to form a lively picture.
NOTES Not the most exciting geranium, but it has a long flowering season and the blooms are distinctive and attractive. Cut it back in midseason if the stems become too long and straggly; it will regrow and reflower.

Geranium 'Ann Folkard'. ▲

A large billowing and mounding plant with chartreuse-yellow leaves that mature to light green. Long, thin, nonrooting stems spread out and clamber through other perennials and small shrubs. The flower petals are magenta, and are rounded with prominent black veins that merge toward the center.

ZONES 5–10, possibly lower
PLANT SIZE 18 × 48 in. (45 × 122 cm)
SOIL Well-drained, slightly acidic to neutral to slightly alkaline
LIGHT Morning sun and afternoon shade; in the hot sun you can shelter it between two taller perennials
PROPAGATION Crown division
ORIGIN *G. procurrens* × *G. psilostemon*. Reverend O. Folkard raised the plant in the United Kingdom from seed of the *G. procurrens* cross in 1973.
GARDEN AND DESIGN USES In the front of a large perennial border, hanging over a rock wall, or in a large container
NOTES Will flower from midspring to late summer. It reportedly does not do well in a combination of high heat and humidity, and some gardeners note that it will not overwinter in wet clay soils.

Geranium 'Blue Sunrise'

A large mounding plant with long trailing flowering stems. It is notable for its new growth of yellow leaves, which become yellow-green as the plant ages. The flowers are 1¼ inches (3.1 cm) in diameter, light violet blue, with purple veins, that age to a more pinkish color.

ZONES 5–10
PLANT SIZE 20–36 × 48–60 in. (50–90 × 122–150 cm)
SOIL Well-drained, slightly acidic to neutral to slightly alkaline
LIGHT Full sun in mild summer gardens, morning sun/afternoon shade in hot summer gardens; the yellow leaves will burn in long exposure to hot sun
PROPAGATION Restricted to licensed propagators
ORIGIN Possibly *G. wallichianum* 'Buxton's Variety' × *G.* 'Ann Folkard'. It was found in the nursery of Hans Kramer, Kwerkeri De Hessenhof, Netherlands, in 1994. It was originally known as 'Verguld Saffier' until Blooms of Bressingham patented it in 1999.
GARDEN AND DESIGN USES Its large size requires careful siting in the garden. The best locations might be against a fence or at the front of shrub borders, where it will not engulf other plants.
NOTES Heat and humidity tolerant. Prune it judiciously to keep it under control.

Geranium 'Anne Thomson'

A large mounding plant, more compact than G. 'Ann Folkard' and with shorter trailing stems. It has distinctive yellow-green leaves, but it is mass produced, so there may be some reversion of the leaves to all green. Flowers are magenta with thin black veins and a dark eye, slightly smaller than those on 'Ann Folkard'.

ZONES 5–10, possibly lower
PLANT SIZE 24 × 48 in. (60 × 122 cm)
SOIL Well-drained, slightly acidic to neutral to slightly alkaline
LIGHT Morning sun, afternoon shade
PROPAGATION Crown division
ORIGIN *G. procurrens* × *G. psilostemon*. Alan Bremner raised this in the United Kingdom, and named it for Anne Thomson in 1992.
GARDEN AND DESIGN USES In the middle to front of a shrub or perennial border. The leaves are large but the flowers are not profuse, so it is not a particularly interesting plant for a container.

Geranium christensenianum

Leaves are dark, slightly olive green, and broadly five-lobed. It has long stoloniferous stems which root at their nodes, and small white flowers with prominent purple veins and dark anthers.

ZONES 6–9, below this unknown
PLANT SIZE 8 × 36 in. (20 × 90 cm)
SOIL Well-drained loam, slightly acidic to neutral
LIGHT Morning sun to light shade
PROPAGATION Crown division, seed
ORIGIN Introduced into cultivation from Sichuan, China, and Dan Hinkley distributed it at Heronswood Nursery, Washington, in the 1990s.
GARDEN AND DESIGN USES Ground cover for shade areas that are not otherwise cultivated.

Geranium 'Dilys'

A ground cover for large bare areas. Its foliage is similar to *G. sanguineum*, with a basal mound of dark green small, narrowly dissected leaves and long trailing stems that lie flat on the ground but do not root. It is a large, sprawling low mound. The flowers are red-purple with fine red veins, borne singly or in pairs toward the ends of the stems. Like its parent, *G. sanguineum*, it has a long flowering period.

ZONES 7–10
PLANT SIZE 10–15 × 36–48 in. (25–38 × 90–122 cm)
SOIL Well-drained, slightly acidic to neutral to slightly alkaline
LIGHT Full sun to morning sun and afternoon shade
PROPAGATION Crown division
ORIGIN *G. sanguineum* × *G. procurrens*. Named after Dilys Davies, a member of the Hardy Plant Society in the United Kingdom, and hybridized by Alan Bremner in the Orkney Islands, United Kingdom. Axletree Nursery, United Kingdom, introduced it in 1991.
GARDEN AND DESIGN USES This plant has inherited fall color from its parent, *G. sanguineum*, and its ground-covering capabilities make it useful for intractable areas of the garden, although you can also use it in the front of large perennial borders.
NOTES Take care when pruning the flowering stems. Many of the flowers are borne at the end of the stems, so overenthusiastic pruning may greatly reduce flowering. Cut back to the crown to tidy it up in early spring (or late fall in mild winter areas).

Geranium 'Dragon Heart'

Forms a mound of deep green large, five to seven broadly lobed leaves with very long and trailing flowering stems. It has 2½-inch (6 cm) magenta flowers with black veins that coalesce to a central brownish black eye. Although no geranium flowers are more than 3 inches (7.5 cm) in diameter, 'Dragon Heart' flowers seem particularly large, probably because of their dramatic color.

ZONES 5–9
PLANT SIZE 12 × 36–48 in. (30 × 90–122 cm)
SOIL Well-drained, somewhat moist, slightly acidic to neutral to slightly alkaline
LIGHT Full sun in mild summer gardens, morning sun and afternoon shade in hot summer gardens
PROPAGATION Crown division
ORIGIN *G. psilostemon* × *G.* ×*oxonianum*. A hybrid from Alan Bremner, Orkney Islands, United Kingdom. Fairweather Nursery, United Kingdom, released it in 2006.
GARDEN AND DESIGN USES Trail through other plants in a perennial or shrub border, or in combination with other perennials in a large container.
NOTES Flowering is sometimes reduced in hot summer gardens. Placing it in partial shade may help.

Geranium 'Khan'

Forms a large sprawling mound and looks like a very large *G. sanguineum*, with deep green fingered leaves. The flowers are purple-red and 2 inches (5 cm) in diameter.

ZONES 4–10

PLANT SIZE 30–36 × 36–40 in. (75–90 × 90–102 cm)

SOIL Will tolerate many different types of soil, clay, loam, and sand, and is drought tolerant when established. Soil can be neutral to slightly acidic.

LIGHT Full sun

PROPAGATION Root division

ORIGIN Possibly *G. sanguineum* × *G. wlassovianum*. Allan Robinson raised it at the Royal Horticultural Society Gardens, Wisley, United Kingdom, and The Hardy Plant Society Geranium Group News, United Kingdom, first published it in 1997.

GARDEN AND DESIGN USES Use as a filler for large areas that are difficult to plant. Water through the first season to establish.

Geranium lambertii

Forms a low mound with few basal leaves and long trailing flowering stems. The leaves have five sharply pointed lobes and are slightly wrinkled. By far the most distinctive feature is the nodding, saucer-shaped flowers, which are pale pink.

ZONES 6–8
PLANT SIZE 12 × 24–36 in. (30 × 60–90 cm)
SOIL Well-drained, moist
LIGHT Morning sun and afternoon shade, light dappled shade in mild summer gardens only
PROPAGATION Seed, crown division
ORIGIN Nepal, Bhutan, Tibet, North India, Kashmir, Pakistan
GARDEN AND DESIGN USES A stunning plant for a mild coastal garden. Give it a raised area where visitors can admire the flowers, or grow it in a container where the long flowering stems can be supported.
NOTES Does not like hot dry summers or poor drainage. It is sometimes reluctant to flower. If you like a challenge, *G. lambertii* is for you.

CULTIVARS

***G. lambertii* 'Swansdown'** ▲ 12 × 24–36 in. (30 × 60–90 cm). Richard Clifton, United Kingdom, named it in 1979. The name is applied to a form that has mottled green leaves and white flowers with a red center and green veins. It comes true from seed.

HYBRIDS

G. 'Coombland White'
G. 'Joy'
G. 'Salome'

Geranium 'Perfect Storm'

Soft gray-green leaves with five lobes on a prostrate spreading plant. Vivid medium lavender-rose flowers with a black eye and prominent black veins.

ZONES 5–9
PLANT SIZE 10 × 24–30 in. (25 × 60–75 cm)
SOIL Well-drained loam, slightly acidic to neutral
LIGHT Morning sun and afternoon shade, particularly in hot summer gardens
PROPAGATION Crown division
ORIGIN A four-way cross Alan Bremner made in the Orkney Islands, United Kingdom, in 2006, using *G. traversii*, *G. sessiliflorum*, and two unknown geraniums.
GARDEN AND DESIGN USES Over walls and in containers
NOTES Needs to be cut back annually, as the long flowering stems get straggly. It flowers spring through fall.

Geranium 'Pink Penny'

Forms a mound of medium green faintly marbled, three- to five-lobed basal leaves with long trailing flowering stems. It has cup-shaped deep pink flowers with an almost white center, purple veins, and sooty anthers.

ZONES 5–9
PLANT SIZE 15–18 × 36–48 in. (38–45 × 90–122 cm)
SOIL Slightly moist and free draining loam, sandy, or clay soil; will withstand dryish soil when mature
LIGHT Full sun in mild summers, morning sun and afternoon shade in hot summer gardens.
PROPAGATION Restricted to licensed propagators
ORIGIN Possibly *G. wallichianum* 'Syabru' × *G.* 'Jolly Bee' (a former Dutch hybrid that has been replaced by *G.* 'Rozanne'). A seedling from a breeding program by Marco van Noort, Netherlands, designed to develop pink-flowered hybrids from *G. wallichianum*. It was patented in 2007.
GARDEN AND DESIGN USES In containers, over walls, on slopes or in the front of shrub or perennial borders
NOTES Trim back during the growing season if it looks untidy, and it will regrow leaves and new flowering stems. All *G. wallichianum* selections tend to lose leaves from the flowering stems during hot summers.

Geranium procurrens

A low ground cover with very long flowering stems. It will throw itself over shrubs, perennials, and paths that are in the way. The leaves are lightly marbled. Its most distinctive feature is that it roots along the nodes of the stems. The flowers are light lavender-purple with purple-black centers.

ZONES 7–9
PLANT SIZE 12–18 × 60 in. (30–45 × 150 cm) or more
SOIL Moist loam, slightly acidic to neutral
LIGHT Morning sun and afternoon shade
PROPAGATION Seed or nodal cuttings
ORIGIN East Nepal and Sikkim, high-altitude valleys and forests
GARDEN AND DESIGN USES Use a certain amount of caution when planting, as it is probably suitable only in wild gardens. However, the plant is easy to grow, its flowers are attractive, and it works well as a ground cover.
HYBRIDS
G. 'Ann Folkard'
G. 'Salome'

Geranium 'Salome'

Forms a small mound with long trailing flowering stems and has a small crown of yellow leaves that become yellow-green as the growing season advances. The leaves have five broad and deep lobes. The flowers are a distinctive pale violet with dark purple veins and a very large dark center, which contrasts beautifully with the yellow foliage. There are gaps between the spoon-shaped petals.

ZONES 6–9
SOIL Light loam, slightly moist, slightly acidic to neutral
LIGHT Morning sun and afternoon shade in all but the mildest summer gardens
PLANT SIZE 12–18 × 36–48 in. (30–45 × 90–122 cm)
PROPAGATION Crown division; some growers have suggested that you can also divide the plant by stem cuttings
ORIGIN Possibly *G. lambertii* × *G. procurrens*. Elizabeth Strangman raised a seedling at Washfield Nursery, United Kingdom, in 1981.
GARDEN AND DESIGN USES As a ground cover or draped over a wall. If it starts to look untidy in midseason, cut it back to the crown and it will releaf and reflower.
NOTES Attractively wends its way through surrounding vegetation. It will flower from late spring through fall. It seems to do better in cool summers with some protection from hot afternoon sun.

Geranium 'Sandrine'

A large mound of gold basal leaves and long trailing flowering stems bearing vivid magenta flowers with black veins and a large black center, slightly less than 2 inches (5 cm) wide. The gold color of the leaves is stronger than on G. 'Ann Folkard' and remains a little longer before it changes to yellow-green.

ZONES 5–9
PLANT SIZE 18 × 30 in. (45 × 75 cm)
SOIL Good drainage, slightly moist, slightly acidic to neutral to slightly alkaline
LIGHT Morning sun and afternoon shade in all but the mildest summer gardens
PROPAGATION Restricted to licensed propagators
ORIGIN Possibly G. 'Ann Folkard' × G. 'Patricia'. Thierry Delabroye developed this in France before 2006 and named it after his wife. It was patented in 2007.
NOTES You can cut it back midseason for another flush of gold leaves, and it will usually develop new flowering stems.

Geranium 'Sweet Heidy'

A mounding habit with long sprawling flowering stems and medium green leaves that are lightly marbled with a yellow-green center, three to five lobes, and strong veining. It has a typical G. wallichianum flower with a large pale center and changing rainbow of outer rings that vary from pink to purple as the flowers age.

ZONES 5–10
PLANT SIZE 15 × 15–20 in. (38 × 38–50 cm)
SOIL Light loam, moist, neutral to slightly alkaline
LIGHT Morning sun to partial shade
PROPAGATION Restricted to licensed propagators
ORIGIN Possibly G. wallichianum and another unknown G. wallichianum selection. Marco van Noort, Netherlands, bred this and named it for his wife.
GARDEN AND DESIGN USES A trailing plant for a garden wall, a steep slope, or a large container
NOTES Does not start flowering until late spring and continues through late fall.

Geranium thunbergii 'Jester's Jacket'

Forms a mound of cream-colored leaves with green, red and white dots and splashes. The leaves have five broadly lobed and separated divisions, and it has small pale pink flowers. It is the good child of its very scary parent, *G. thunbergii*. The green form of *G. thunbergii* is invasive; do not cultivate it. However, 'Jester's Jacket' is attractive and well behaved, and the leaf color provides an interesting contrast in a garden.

ZONES 4–9
PLANT SIZE 12 × 18 in. (30 × 45 cm)
SOIL Moist and well-drained, acidic to alkaline
LIGHT Morning sun and afternoon shade
PROPAGATION Seed
ORIGIN Plant World Seeds, United Kingdom, introduced this in 2002. It appears to come true from seed.
GARDEN AND DESIGN USES An accent plant in perennial gardens and containers

Geranium 'Tiny Monster'

Low growing and sprawling from a small crown, a bit like custard spilled on a flat surface. The trailing stems are very long and will cover quite a large area in one season. The leaves are dark green and fingered. The flowers are a deep medium pink with dark purple-red veins, about 1½ inches (3.8 cm) in diameter.

ZONES 4–9; heat and humidity tolerant
PLANT SIZE 12 × 36–48 in. (30 × 90–122 cm)
SOIL Well-drained to dryish loam, mildly acidic to neutral
LIGHT Full sun to light shade
PROPAGATION Crown division

ORIGIN Possibly *G. sanguineum* 'Ankum's Pride' × *G. psilostemon*, a hybrid raised by Rolf Offenthal, Germany, and published in 1999.
GARDEN AND DESIGN USES Do not use this ground cover near any choice little rarity.
NOTES Flowers heavily in spring and sporadically during the summer, often near the tips of the flower stems. It is heat and humidity tolerant in the American South. The name is an advertising triumph, as hardly anyone can resist buying it. Fortunately, the plant is sterile and can be sheared back, so the 'Monster' should evoke only a mild shudder.

Geranium wallichianum

Forms a small crown with long trailing flowering stems and leaves that are lightly marbled. The leaves are three- to five-lobed, deeply cut, and toothed. It tends to lose its basal rosette of leaves as it grows, so it can look straggly. The flowers are very variable in color from pink and lavender to light blue and purple, with dark veins and mostly, but not exclusively, a large pale center. They are 1¼ inches (3.1 cm) wide, upturned, and almost flat.

ZONES 5–9
PLANT SIZE 15 × 24–36 in. (38 × 60–90 cm)
SOIL Lightly moist and free-draining loam, slightly acidic to neutral to slightly alkaline
LIGHT Morning sun to full sun in mild summer gardens, light shade in hot summers
PROPAGATION Crown division, seed
ORIGIN From the Himalayas, northeast Afghanistan, Kashmir, and Bhutan, between 7800 and 12,000 feet (2380–3650 m) elevation. It was introduced to Europe in 1820.
GARDEN AND DESIGN USES The flowering stems tend to lose leaves, so it is sometimes useful to grow this through other plants. Use it in perennial borders, over walls, and in large containers.
NOTES Flowers late in the season and will carry on blooming until the frost. A number of color selections have been given cultivar names.
CULTIVARS
G. wallichianum **'Azurro'** ▲ 18 × 24 in. (45 × 60 cm). Marco van Noort, Netherlands, introduced the plant in 2010. It has lavender-blue flowers with dark veins and a pale center.
G. wallichianum **'Buxton's Variety'** (syn. *G. wallichianum* 'Buxton's Blue') 15–18 × 24–36 in. (38–45 × 60–90 cm). Appeared in the garden of E. C. Buxton, North Wales, in the 1920s. It has small compact crowns with long trailing flowering stems. The flowers are light blue with a white center. Seedlings come mostly true, but should be selected for the best blue color.

G. wallichianum 'Buxton's Pink' 15–18 × 24 in. (38–45 × 60 cm). Thompson and Morgan, United Kingdom, raised this seedling in 2000. It has medium green broad-lobed leaves that are slightly fuzzy. Its flowers are lilac-pink with numerous dark purple veins and sooty anthers.

G. wallichianum 'Crystal Lake' ◄ 15 × 24–30 in. (38 × 45–60 cm). A seedling of *G. wallichianum* 'Silver Blue' that comes from Kwerkerij De Hessenhof and Hans Kramer of the Netherlands. It grows pale icy blue flowers with dark purple veins that coalesce in the center of the flower and dark pollen. It is a mounding plant with long trailing flowering stems. It flowers in summer to late fall. Recommended for window boxes, over low walls, and containers.

Morning sun is best, but full sun in mild summer gardens and afternoon shade in hot summer gardens work. If it is grown in too much hot sun it can get scraggly while the leaves tend to burn and fall off the flowering stems. Restricted to licensed propagators.

G. wallichianum 'Rise and Shine' 8 × 25 in. (20 × 65 cm). Marco van Noort, Netherlands, raised this in 2007 and patented it in 2012. The flowers have pale centers and change color from purple-violet to purple through the length of the petals. It is sterile. Restricted to licensed propagators.

G. wallichianum 'Shocking Blue' ▶ 15 × 36 in. (38 × 90 cm). From Sugar Creek Gardens, Missouri, in 2007. It has large lavender flowers that tend to turn pink-blue in hot sun. The white center, although large, is not well defined. It has a mound of basal leaves and long trailing flowering stems.

G. wallichianum 'Syabru' 12 × 24 in. (30 × 60 cm). Edward Needham collected this in Nepal and named it for the village in which he found it. Washfield Nursery, United Kingdom, introduced it in 1991. The flowers are a deep pink with dark veins, and slightly smaller than *G. wallichianum* 'Buxton's Variety'. There is no white eye.

G. wallichianum 'Sylvia's Surprise' 15 × 30 in. (38 × 75 cm). Sylvia Morrow discovered this in her garden, and Blooms of Bressingham patented in 2009. Flowers are pink with pale centers, 1½ to 2 inches (3.8–5 cm) wide. It flowers on and off during the summer and continues into the late fall as the weather cools. The leaves have good autumn color. Like all *G. wallichianum* selections, it needs protection from hot afternoon summer sun. Restricted to licensed propagators.

HYBRIDS

***G.* 'Azure Rush'**

***G.* 'Blue Sunrise'**

***G.* 'Havana Blues'** It is a cultivar of *G. wallichianum*, although its specific parentage is not known. It is compact at 12 × 15 in. (30 × 38 cm). Leaves have five lobes and are marbled in light yellow when young, which becomes yellow-green marbling as the leaves mature. The flowers are 2½ inches (6 cm) and light lavender with prominent violet veins that coalesce into a red-purple blotch near the base, which is almost white. The anthers are sooty black. Reportedly useful for high-temperature gardens in the American South and Southwest.

***G.* 'Pink Penny'**

***G.* 'Rosetta'** Parentage *G. wallichianum* 'Syabru' × unknown parent. 15 × 24–30 in. (38 × 45–75 cm). Hans Kramer, Netherlands, discovered this in 2001. The 1¼-inch (3.1 cm) flowers are deep pink with reddish veins and a pale zone in the center. They have notched and separated petals shaped like spoons. The flowering stems are rosy pink and the large leaves are olive green.

***G.* 'Rozanne'**

***G.* 'Sweet Heidy'**

Geranium wlassovianum

A large mounding plant with long flowering stems. The leaves are shallowly dissected and have five to seven broad lobes, and are purple-brown as they emerge from dormancy in the spring. As the leaves mature, they become gray-green and then take on tones of cinnamon and red in the fall. Flowers are purple with dark veins and a small white center.

ZONES 4–9
PLANT SIZE 12–18 × 36 in. (30–45 × 90 cm)
SOIL Well-drained, moist, slightly acidic to neutral to slightly alkaline
LIGHT Morning sun/afternoon shade to full sun in mild summer areas
PROPAGATION Crown division, seed
ORIGIN The plant has a wide area of distribution from eastern Siberia, Mongolia, into northern China.
GARDEN AND DESIGN USES Perennial borders, containers, slopes
NOTES Tolerates heat and humidity, and flowers summer through fall.
HYBRIDS
G. 'Lakwijk Star' Parentage *G. wlassovianum* × unknown parent. 15 × 24–36 in. (38 × 60–90 cm). This was originally known as *G.* 'Lyona', and then *G.* 'Lakwijk Star' after 2003. It has the gray-green leaves of *G. wlassovianum* and large purple flowers with dark veins. Plants available in the United States look very similar to the species. It has good fall color. It is named for Jan van Lakwijk, Netherlands, who raised it.

Geranium yesoense

A bushy mound with rhizomatous roots and long stems. Leaves are sharply and deeply cut into seven lobes. The flowers are pink or white and around 1 inch (2.5 cm) in diameter.

ZONES 5–9
PLANT SIZE 12 × 30 in. (30 × 75 cm)
SOIL Well-drained loam, neutral to slightly acidic
LIGHT Dappled sun to light shade
ORIGIN Hokkaido and Honshu, Japan
GARDEN AND DESIGN USES It is not of great horticultural interest, except as a possible low-growing ground cover in a light shade border.
PROPAGATION Crown division, seed
NOTES Seems to be a tough garden plant, but it can grow untidy. Trim it back at least once per year.
FORMS
G. yesoense var. *nipponicum* ▲ 12 × 30 in. (30 × 75 cm). There are only slight botanical differences separating var. *nipponicum* from var. *yesoense*, relating to the stem and flower stems being less hairy or without long hairs. This variety has pale pink flowers.

BORDERS AND BEDDING

A large number of hardy geraniums are suitable for use in perennial borders and bedding schemes in combination with other perennials, roses, and small shrubs. They are successful in moderately fertile loamy garden soils, either mildly acidic to neutral, and either full sun or partial sun. Mild summer gardens, where daytime high temperatures remain moderate, usually around 80°F (27°C) or lower, are suitable for almost all the hardy geraniums in this section. Plants should be given afternoon shade in hot summer gardens where daytime temperatures are above 80°F (27°C) for long periods of time.

Geranium aristatum

Makes mounds of dark green softly hairy leaves that are seven-lobed and toothed. It has nodding flowers with reflexed petals of white to pale lilac, with lilac veins that coalesce into a lilac center at the base of the petals. The flowers look like small Regency striped shuttlecocks.

ZONES 5–9
PLANT SIZE 15 × 20 in. (38 × 50 cm)
SOIL Moderately moist loam, slightly acidic to neutral
LIGHT Partial shade
PROPAGATION Crown division, seed (although the plant produces very few seeds)
ORIGIN Mountains of southern Albania, southern Balkans, and northwestern Greece
GARDEN AND DESIGN USES Place in light shade gardens with plants whose season of bloom follows to provide extended visual interest.
NOTES Has a concentrated season of bloom in the late spring, then remains a mound of leaves for the rest of the growing season.

Geranium asphodeloides

Large mounds of medium green rounded, deeply five- to seven-lobed leaves. It is variable in leaf shape, depending on the subspecies, but all forms have rounded leaves with lobes that are dissected from more than half to nearly all of the leaf blade. Large masses of small starry flowers of white or pale to deep pink, often with prominent veins, 1 inch (2.5 cm) wide. The flowering stems are 12 to 24 inches (30 × 60 cm) long.

ZONES 5–9
PLANT SIZE 12–18 × 15–24 in. (30–45 × 38–60 cm)
SOIL Moderately moist loam, mildly acidic to neutral
LIGHT Sun in mild summer gardens, morning sun and afternoon shade in hot summer gardens
PROPAGATION Crown division, seed
ORIGIN Southern Europe from Sicily eastward to Turkey, Lebanon, Syria, northern Iran, and the Caucasus. It is found in grassland, rocky slopes, scrub, and forest.
GARDEN AND DESIGN USES Perennial borders
NOTES You can cut back the plant to just above the crown after the main flush of flowers, and it will grow new leaves and new flowering stems in the same season. If you don't do this, seedlings can become a problem.

SUBSPECIES

G. asphodeloides subsp. *asphodeloides* Native to southern Europe from Sicily eastward to Crimea and Caucasus, northern Iran, Turkey. 18 × 20 in. (45 × 50 cm). Green rounded, shallowly toothed leaves that have five to seven broad lobes. The flowers range from pale to deep pink, with darker veins, and the petals are separated.

G. asphodeloides subsp. *crenophilum* From Lebanon and Syria. 12 × 15 in. (30 × 38 cm). Leaves are medium green, large, rounded, and divided into nine lobes. The flowers have deep pink wide petals.

G. asphodeloides subsp. *sintesii* From northern Turkey. 17 × 24 in. (43 × 60 cm). Leaves are medium green, rounded, and covered with red-tipped glandular hairs. The flowers range from pale pink to purple and the petals do not quite overlap.

CULTIVARS

G. asphodeloides subsp. *asphodeloides* 'Prince Regent' ▲ 17 × 24 in. (43 × 60 cm). Axletree Nursery, United Kingdom, introduced this in 1990. It has medium green shallowly rounded, seven-lobed leaves. The pale lilac flowers with dark veins are quite small, so locate the plant close to a path or edging for visitors to enjoy.

G. asphodeloides 'Gorer's Pink' 12 × 20 in. (30 × 50 cm). Named after Richard Gorer, from a collection made in 1974 in the lower part of Mount Pindus in Greece. It has medium green shallowly rounded leaves with seven lobes. The red-pink flowers appear in late spring and early summer, and the plant remains a mound of leaves for the remainder of the growing season.

HYBRIDS

G. asphodeloides subsp. *asphodeloides* × *G. asphodeloides* subsp. *crenophilum* 'Starlight' 18 × 24 in. (45 × 60 cm). Axletree Nursery, United Kingdom, introduced this in 1990 from a selection by Peter Yeo in 1980. The light green leaves are hairy and not as deeply divided as the other selections. It has pure white broad, petalled flowers. Bloom is prolific, and it is a beautiful and effective late spring-flowering plant for a pink and white garden.

Geranium 'Azure Rush'

Forms a low-mounding, slightly sprawling geranium. It branches well and the plant looks full. The green leaves are slightly marbled, broadly seven lobed, deeply dissected, and sharply toothed. The flowers are 2½ inches (6 cm) in diameter, and are a lighter lavender-pink version of G. 'Rozanne', with purple veins.

ZONES 5–9
PLANT SIZE 15 × 24 in. (38 × 60 cm)
SOIL Well-drained loamy soil, slightly acidic to neutral to slightly alkaline
LIGHT Morning sun and afternoon shade in hot summer gardens, full sun in mild summer gardens
PROPAGATION Restricted to licensed propagators
ORIGIN A sport of G. 'Rozanne', one of the most successful geraniums ever hybridized. It has shorter internodes, so it does not spread as far. It was selected in Germany in 2007 from a population of G. 'Rozanne', and patented in 2010.
GARDEN AND DESIGN USES Flower beds, borders, containers, window boxes
NOTES Purchase mature plants. All plants are tissue cultured, so for the first couple of years out of the laboratory growth tends to be slow. It has a very long flowering period, from mid-spring through until frost, and is easy to grow. You can cut back plants to above the crown in spring before growth starts to promote a full appearance in the summer. Gardeners who have grown G. 'Rozanne' might like this paler color echo for variety.

Geranium 'Blue Blood'

Large mounds of medium green hairy, seven-lobed leaves that are overlapping, toothed, and deeply divided. Large deep-purple flowers with almost-black veins and a small white center. Good fall foliage color in cold climates.

ZONES 5–9
PLANT SIZE 20 × 18 in. (50 × 45 cm)
SOIL Moderately damp loam, sandy soil, amended clay, slightly acidic to neutral
LIGHT Full sun in mild summer gardens, morning sun and afternoon shade in hot summer gardens
PROPAGATION Crown division
ORIGIN Possibly *G. gymnocaulon* × *G. ibericum* subsp. *jubatum*. It was a hybrid produced by Robin Moss, United Kingdom.
GARDEN AND DESIGN USES Perennial borders, containers
NOTES Flowers early, so plant with geraniums that flower later, such as *G.* ×*magnificum* 'Rosemoor' to extend the season.

Geranium 'Blue Cloud'

A large clumping perennial that forms tall, loose mounds of finely divided leaves that have five narrow wedge-shaped lobes. It is aptly named for its clouds of light blue flowers with dark purple veins.

ZONES 5–9
PLANT SIZE 36–48 × 36–48 in. (90–122 × 90–122 cm)
SOIL Moderately fertile, slightly acidic to neutral to slightly alkaline
LIGHT Full sun in mild summer gardens, morning sun and afternoon shade in hot summer gardens
PROPAGATION Crown division
ORIGIN Possibly a seedling of *G.* 'Nimbus'. Found at Axletree Nursery, United Kingdom, in 1994.
GARDEN AND DESIGN USES Use it in the midsection of a perennial border, and as a ground cover in the light sun to dappled shade provided by high pruned trees and shrubs.
NOTES If you cut back the plant after it finishes flowering in midsummer, it will regrow and reflower to a lesser degree in the late summer.

Geranium 'Blue Robin'▾

A large mounding plant with medium green leaves that have five toothed, broad, and shallow lobes with a pebbled surface. It grows from large rhizomatous roots. Its large 2-inch (5 cm) flowers are violet-blue and filled with purple veins. The petals are spoon shaped, notched, and separated from each other.

ZONES 5–9
PLANT SIZE 18–20 × 24 in. (45–50 × 60 cm)
SOIL Moderately moist loam, sandy soil or moist amended clay, slightly acidic to neutral
LIGHT Full sun in mild summer gardens, morning sun and afternoon shade in hot summer gardens
PROPAGATION Crown division
ORIGIN Possibly *G. renardii* × *G. platypetalum* 'Turco'. A chance seedling found in the garden of Karen Wouters, Kwekerij voor Vaste Planten, Hijkersmilde, Netherlands, in 2001, and published by Geraniaceae Nursery, California.
GARDEN AND DESIGN USES Perennial gardens, containers

Geranium 'Blushing Turtle'▾

Forms mounds of evergreen foliage in mild climates. The medium green leaves have good fall color and are somewhat similar to *G. sanguineum*, but with broader leaf divisions. The flowers are medium pink with purple veins and are 1½ inches (3.8 cm) in diameter.

ZONES 5–10
PLANT SIZE 18 × 36 in. (45 × 90 cm)
SOIL Well-drained, moderately moist, medium loam, slightly acidic to neutral to slightly alkaline
LIGHT Full sun in mild summer gardens, morning sun and afternoon shade in hot summer gardens
PROPAGATION Restricted to licensed propagators
ORIGIN Possibly *G. sanguineum* × *G. ×oxonianum* 'Julie Brennan' or an unnamed selection of *G. asphodeloides*. Karin Kosick hybridized this in British Columbia, Canada, in 2002.
GARDEN AND DESIGN USES Perennial borders, a ground cover in morning sun areas, on the top of walls, climbing through shrubs
NOTES Very easy to grow and looks neat and tidy during the growing season. Flowers heavily in late spring and early summer, with repeat flowering in the early fall.

Geranium 'Brookside'◄

Forms a large, tall clump in the garden with medium green leaves that are narrowly five lobed and dissected to the base with further narrow divisions. It has violet-blue flowers with a small white center.

ZONES 5–9
PLANT SIZE 30–36 × 24–36 in. (75–90 × 60–90 cm)
SOIL Well-drained, reasonably fertile soil, slightly acidic to neutral to slightly alkaline
LIGHT Full sun in mild summer gardens, morning sun and afternoon shade in hot summer gardens
PROPAGATION Crown division
ORIGIN *G. pratense* × *G. clarkei* 'Kashmir Purple'. The plant was found in the experimental beds at Cambridge University Botanic Garden, United Kingdom, in the 1970s, and Peter Yeo selected it. It was named after the house in which the garden offices were based, and Axletree Nursery, United Kingdom, distributed it in 1989. It is widely available in the United States.
GARDEN AND DESIGN USES This is a workhorse in the garden. Plant it in drifts in large natural areas, in groups in perennial borders, or in bright shrub borders. You can also plant it in large containers, or hang it over walls.
NOTES Flower color will change with temperature, particularly in hot days in the summer. Flowers appear more blue in early morning and early evening. Young plants have a tendency to flop over, so stake them or plant close to other tall perennials. They will become more self-supporting as they age. You can also cut them back in midseason to promote new leaves and new flowering stems. Tim Fuller from The Plantsman's Preference, United Kingdom, has noted that *G.* 'Brookside', *G.* 'Orion', and *G.* 'Nimbus' all grow new leaves from the center of the plant, and after flowering you can cut back the old leaves and flowering stems around the outside of the center.
CULTIVARS
G. **'Blue Pearl'** A selected seedling of *G.* 'Brookside' from Axletree Nursery, United Kingdom. It is described as having "bowl-shaped flowers of an unusual pearly medium gray-blue."
HYBRIDS
G. **'Orion'**

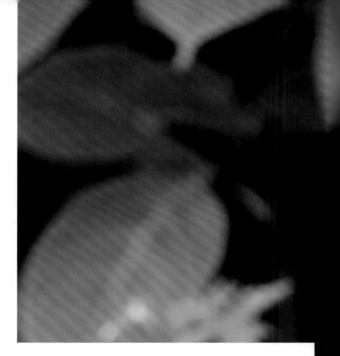

Geranium clarkei

It has seven deeply divided, pinnately lobed, finely dissected, and toothed medium green leaves. The plant has spreading underground rhizomatous roots and forms large loose mounds. The flowers range in color from mauve and purple to white.

ZONES 4–9
PLANT SIZE 24 × 24 in. (60 × 60 cm)
SOIL Moderately moist loam, neutral to slightly alkaline
LIGHT Full sun in mild summer gardens; not suitable for hot summer gardens
PROPAGATION Crown division
ORIGIN Kashmir, occurring naturally between 6800 and 13,700 feet (2075–4175 m).
GARDEN AND DESIGN USES Perennial borders, containers
NOTES Flowers heavily in the late spring, after which the plants can be cut down to just above the crown and new leaves and flowering stems will form. Unfortunately, it does not do particularly well in areas with high summer heat or high humidity; grow this plant in a garden with relatively cool summers.

CULTIVARS
G. clarkei **'Kashmir Purple'** 24 × 24 in. (60 × 60 cm). G. S. Thomas named it at the 1976 Royal Horticultural Society trial, Wisley, United Kingdom. Other purple forms of *G. clarkei* are not named. 'Kashmir Purple' has medium green finely divided, seven-lobed leaves and strong mauve-purple flowers. It blooms in early summer and often has sporadic flowers later in the season.

G. clarkei **'Kashmir White'** 24 × 24 in. (60 × 60 cm). Probably the loveliest of all the *G. clarkei* selections. It has 2-inch (5 cm) white flowers with lavender veins. Although it tends to flower in late spring and early summer, cutting the plant back to the ground and fertilizing will often provoke a second bloom.

G. clarkei **'Mount Stewart'** 12 × 18 in. (30 × 45 cm). From the National Trust garden at Mount Stewart in Northern Ireland, and distributed by Axletree Nursery, United Kingdom, in 1995. Its original provenance is in question. The flowers are white with an almost indiscernible pink flush and deep pink veins that coalesce into a medium pink blotch at the base of the petals. The plant resembles 'Kashmir White' in other details.

HYBRIDS
G. **'Brookside'**
G. **'Kashmir Blue'** ▶ Parentage possibly *G. pratense* f. *albiflorum* × *G. clarkei* 'Kashmir White'. 20–24 × 24 in. (50–60 × 60 cm). From De Bloemenhoek Nursery, Netherlands, in 1990. Ivan Louette, Belgium, raised it in the mid-1980s. The plant resembles *G. pratense* in size and leaf, but the flowers are large and pale blue.
G. **'Kashmir Green'** Parentage possibly *G. clarkei* × *G. pratense*. 18 × 24 in. (45 × 60 cm). From Coen Jansen, Vaste Planten, Netherlands, in 2000. It is slightly more substantial than *G. clarkei* and somewhat more like *G. pratense*. It is described as having white flowers with green veins and a small green eye.
G. **'Kashmir Pink'**
G. **'Natalie'** Parentage *G. clarkei* 'Kashmir White' × *G. saxatile*. 18–20 × 24 in. (45–50 × 60 cm). This Alan Bremner hybrid was first published in 1996 and introduced by Judith Bradshaw, Catforth Gardens, United Kingdom, in 1997. It is named for her granddaughter. Leaves are finely dissected and the lobes are narrow. The flowers are a soft blue with a small light center and black anthers. It flowers profusely and quite early in the season. If you cut it back after flowering, it may have a second bloom if the weather remains cool.
G. **'Nimbus'**

Geranium 'Coombland White'

Mounding perennial with green marbled, rounded, seven-lobed leaves. Flowers are very pale pink with purple veins. They face upward and become white with age.

ZONES 5–9
PLANT SIZE 15 × 18 in. (38 × 45 cm)
SOIL Moderately moist to somewhat dry loam, slightly acidic to neutral; does not do well in heavy clay soils
LIGHT Full sun in mild summer gardens
PROPAGATION Crown division
ORIGIN Possibly *G. lambertii* × *G. traversii*. From Coombland Gardens, United Kingdom, and raised by Rosemary Lee in 1991.
GARDEN AND DESIGN USES Perennial borders, containers
NOTES Not a good choice for a hot summer garden.

Geranium 'Coquet Island'

Has a mound of leaves that are yellow-green to light green, strongly veined, and divided into five broad lobes with shallow and rounded teeth. The flowers are deep blue with a pale zone near the center. The zone has a reddish line around it, and prominent purple veins.

ZONES 5–10
PLANT SIZE 12 × 15 in. (30 × 38 cm)
SOIL Moderately moist loam, slightly acidic to neutral
LIGHT Morning sun and afternoon shade
PROPAGATION Crown division
ORIGIN *G. himalayense* × *G. wallichianum*. Cyril Foster, United Kingdom, bred this and named it after the River Coquet. It was described in 2008 in *Register of Geranium Cultivar Names*.
GARDEN AND DESIGN USES Perennial border, containers
NOTES A very useful compact geranium for the spring and early summer.

Geranium 'Criss Canning'

Mounds of medium green leaves with five to seven broad lobes that are deeply divided with prominent teeth. Profuse violet-blue flowers with purple veins, a hazy reddish central zone, and a small white center.

ZONES 5–9
PLANT SIZE 12–15 × 18 in. (30–38 × 45 cm)
SOIL Moderately moist loam, sandy soil, amended clay, slightly acidic to neutral
LIGHT Full sun in mild summer gardens, morning sun and afternoon shade in hot summer gardens
PROPAGATION Crown division
ORIGIN Possibly *G. pratense* × *G. himalayense*. From David Glenn, Lambley Nursery, Victoria, Australia, in 1997. From mixed *G. pratense* seed his father sent from the United Kingdom. It is named after Glenn's wife, artist Criss Canning.
GARDEN AND DESIGN USES Perennial borders, containers
NOTES Long flowering and tolerates summer heat.

Geranium 'Diva'

A compact mounding plant with medium green seven-lobed leaves that are similar in appearance to *G. sanguineum*. The foliage on the new growth is yellow-green. It has small light magenta flowers. The petals are spoon shaped and separated.

ZONES 5–10
PLANT SIZE 15 × 24 in. (38 × 60 cm)
SOIL Moderately moist to dryish loam, sandy soil, clay with good drainage, neutral to slightly acidic
LIGHT Full sun in mild summer gardens, morning sun and afternoon shade in hot summer gardens
PROPAGATION Crown division, roots
ORIGIN *G. sanguineum* × *G. swatense*. An Alan Bremner hybrid originally distributed by Catforth Gardens, United Kingdom, in 1993.
GARDEN AND DESIGN USES Perennial borders, rock walls

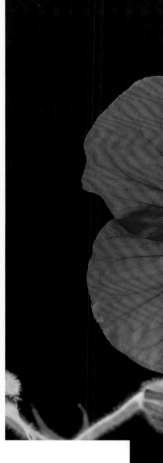

Geranium 'Dreamland' ▲

Mounds of gray-green broadly five-lobed leaves with long flowering stems. Flowers are pale pink and cup shaped, with notched petals, dark veins, and a pale center, 1¼ inches (3.1 cm) in diameter.

ZONES 6–9
PLANT SIZE 12 × 20 in. (30 × 50 cm)
SOIL Moderately moist well-drained loam, slightly acidic to neutral
LIGHT Morning sun and afternoon shade
PROPAGATION Restricted to licensed propagators
ORIGIN *G. traversii* × *G. oxonianum* 'Wageningen.' An Alan Bremner hybrid from 1996.
GARDEN AND DESIGN USES Front of a perennial border, container, ground cover
NOTES Long flowering from spring to fall. It is too soon to predict how it will do in heat and humidity. It appears to be sterile.

Geranium 'Eureka Blue' ▶

Large mounds of medium green deeply dissected leaves and large, deep lavender-blue flowers with magenta veins and a small white eye, 2 inches (5 cm) in diameter.

ZONES 5–9
PLANT SIZE 30–36 × 36–48 in. (75–90 × 90–122 cm)
SOIL Well-drained loam, slightly acidic to neutral
LIGHT Full sun in mild summer gardens, morning sun and afternoon shade in hot summer gardens
PROPAGATION Restricted to licensed propagators
ORIGIN Possibly a sport of *G.* 'Orion' from Brian Kabbes, Netherlands.
GARDEN AND DESIGN USES Perennial border, mass planting for drifts of color, containers
NOTES Flowers late spring to midsummer. Good autumn color in the leaves. Remove spent or long and untidy flowering stems for rebloom.

Geranium 'Eva' ▲

A mounding plant with medium green leaves that have five to seven deeply divided broad lobes. The flowers are large and magenta with black veins and a black center.

ZONES 5–9
PLANT SIZE 18 × 36 in. (45 × 90 cm)
SOIL Moderately moist loam, slightly acidic to neutral
LIGHT Morning sun and afternoon shade
PROPAGATION Crown division
ORIGIN *G. pratense* × *G. psilostemon*. Alan Bremner bred this, and Catforth Gardens, United Kingdom, distributed it in 1994.
GARDEN AND DESIGN USES Perennial borders, containers
NOTES Its long flowering stems look attractive weaving through other clumps of flowers. This plant is a bit more compact than the other selections and hybrids of *G. psilostemon*.

Geranium goldmannii

A large spreading mound with long flowering stems. It has medium green small, rounded, seven-lobed, deeply dissected leaves that have a prominent network of slightly darker-colored veins. The flowers are pale mauve with a pale center. The petals are widely separated at their bases.

ZONES 8–9, possibly lower
PLANT SIZE 15 × 24–36 in. (38 × 60–90 cm)
SOIL Well-drained moderately moist loam, slightly acidic to neutral
LIGHT Full sun in mild summer gardens, morning sun and afternoon shade in hot summer gardens
PROPAGATION Roots, crowns, seed
ORIGIN Chiapas, Mexico
GARDEN AND DESIGN USES Perennial border, containers
NOTES Blooms heavily in the summer and appears to respond to some summer water. It is a handsome addition to a perennial border.

Geranium hayatanum

A bushy, trailing perennial with dark green mottled, hairy leaves that have five narrowly lobed divisions. The leaf blades are cut nearly to the base. It has long trailing flowering stems, and light pink flowers with a white eye and dark purple veins. The peduncles have only one flower, not the usual two.

ZONES 5–9
PLANT SIZE 15 × 20 in. (38 × 50 cm)
SOIL Well-drained loam, neutral to slightly acidic
LIGHT Morning sun to light shade
PROPAGATION Crown division. It hybridizes readily, so it is impossible to know what you have from seeds.
ORIGIN From the mountains of Taiwan, at around 10,800 feet (3300 m). It grows on forest floors, rocky slopes, trailsides, and exposed scree slopes. Bleddyn and Sue Wynn-Jones of Crûg Farm Plants, Wales, found the plant. It does not appear at elevations below 9800 feet (3000 m).
GARDEN AND DESIGN USES Edge of a woodland garden, shrub border

Geranium himalayense

A rhizomatous rooted plant with sparsely toothed leaves that have seven broad lobes. The flowers are deep blue, flushed red at the base, saucer shaped, and 1¾ inches (4.4 cm) in diameter. It is one of the larger-flowered species of hardy geraniums.

ZONES 5–10
PLANT SIZE 15 × 24 in. (38 × 60 cm)
SOIL Moderately fertile and moist garden soil, neutral to mildly acidic
LIGHT Full sun in mild summer gardens, morning sun and afternoon shade in hot summer gardens
PROPAGATION Seed for species, crown division for cultivars
ORIGIN Himalayas from northeastern Afghanistan to central Nepal, Pamir Mountains
GARDEN AND DESIGN USES Perennial border, ground cover
NOTES A very useful ground cover. It spreads through the ground on small wiry roots and appears here and there, gradually covering quite large areas.
CULTIVARS
G. himalayense **'Baby Blue'** ◀ 12 × 18 in. (30 × 45 cm). Axletree Nursery received this from Ingwersen's Nursery, and introduced it in 1994. A compact and very floriferous form of the species. Its large blue flowers, which have a reddish tinge and are covered with light red veins, are 2½ inches (6 cm) in diameter.
G. himalayense **'Derrick Cook'** ▶ 18 × 36 in. (45 × 90 cm). From Nepal, and named after its discoverer in 1984. Its leaves have five broad wedge-shaped lobes with rounded teeth. It has good fall color. The flowers are white with purple veins, saucer shaped, and very large at 2¼-inch (5.7 cm) diameter.

G. himalayense 'Devil's Blue' 12 × 15 in. (30 × 38 cm). A seedling of G. himalayense 'Baby Blue' that Croftway Nursery, United Kingdom, introduced in 1999. The flowers are brilliant blue with purple veins and a faint red halo around a white center, plus wavy petals.

G. himalayense 'Gravetye' ▲ 18 × 24 in. (45 × 60 cm). First published using the name 'Gravetye' by A. T. Johnson in 1937. There appears to be some confusion as to which is the true G. himalayense 'Gravetye'. Peter Yeo describes it as a compact plant having smaller foliage than the species. The flowers are supposed to be 2 inches (5 cm), larger than G. himalayense, with a strong purple flush in the center. There appear to be a number of different forms of G. himalayense distributed under the name 'Gravetye', none of which exactly fits the description, and it is not clear if G. himalayense 'Gravetye' exists in the United States.

G. himalayense 'Irish Blue' 15 × 20 in. (38 × 50 cm). Found in Ireland and named by Graham Stewart Thomas, United Kingdom, in 1947. It has flowers that are a very pale pinkish blue with darker veins, fading toward a pale reddish-blue center. The plant is compact and flowers over a long period. There is a much darker blue-flowered plant in the nursery trade also available under the name of 'Irish Blue'.

G. himalayense 'Plenum' ◄ (syn. G. himalayense 'Birch Double') 18 × 24 in. (45 × 60 cm). This was first listed in the J. Stormonth Catalog, United Kingdom, in 1928. It has the same habit of roaming around on rhizomatous roots as G. himalayense. The leaves are small, and the divisions are short and rounded. The flowers are small, 1¼ inches (3.1 cm) in diameter, double light lavender rosettes that are pinker than the species. The plant is less vigorous than G. himalayense, with fewer flowers.

HYBRIDS

G. 'Coquet Island'

G. 'Rozanne'

Geranium ibericum

It has hairy, nine- to eleven-lobed leaves that are overlapping, acutely toothed, deeply divided, and very large. It is a large spreading plant. The flowers are blue-mauve with light veins, 2 inches (5 cm) in diameter. The differences between the species and subspecies may be of interest to the botanist, but would not be noticed by the gardener.

ZONES 5–10
PLANT SIZE 20 × 36 in. (50 × 90 cm)
SOIL Moderately moist loam, well-drained, slightly acidic to neutral
LIGHT Full sun in mild summer gardens, morning sun and afternoon shade in hot summer gardens
PROPAGATION Crown or root division
ORIGIN Northeastern Turkey, Caucasus
GARDEN AND DESIGN USES Perennial borders, containers
NOTES Flowers heavily in the spring and early summer. If you remove the spent flowering stems, it will flower sporadically throughout the rest of the growing season.

SUBSPECIES
G. ibericum subsp. jubatum ▶ From northeastern Turkey. 15 × 18 in. (38 × 45 cm). It has medium green hairy, nine- to eleven-lobed leaves. The lobes are overlapping and deeply toothed. Glandular hairs on the pedicels distinguish it from G. ibericum subsp. ibericum, but the leaves are very similar in shape. The flowers are small, deep blue-violet, and heavily veined.

CULTIVARS
G. ibericum subsp. jubatum 'White Zigana' ▶ 18 × 20 in. (45 × 50 cm). Michael Baron, United Kingdom, collected it in the Zigana Pass of northeastern Turkey in 1994. It has white flowers, 1½ inches (3.8 cm) in diameter, with notched petals and lilac veins.
G. ibericum 'Ushguli Grijs' 18 × 24 in. (45 × 60 cm). Hans Kramer, Kwerkerij de Hessenhof, found the plant in the Caucasus mountains and introduced it, and Birgitte Husted Bendtsen published it in Storkenaeb in 2003. It sports large gray-blue flowers with purple veins.
HYBRIDS
G. ×magnificum

Geranium 'Ivan' ▲

A large mound with long flowering stems and light green basal leaves that have seven broad lobes. The flowers are a light milky magenta with a prominent brown-black center with some white streaks, from which black veins radiate outward.

ZONES 5–9
PLANT SIZE 24 × 36 in. (60 × 90 cm)
SOIL Moderately moist loam, slightly acidic to neutral
LIGHT Full sun in mild summer gardens, morning sun and afternoon shade in hot summer gardens
PROPAGATION Crown division
ORIGIN Possibly *G. psilostemon* × *G.* ×*oxonianum*. Named for Ivan Louette, Belgium, from De Bloemenhoek, Netherlands, in 1991.
GARDEN AND DESIGN USES Perennial borders, containers
NOTES Along with *G.* 'Eva', this is a somewhat more compact form derived from *G. psilostemon*. It flowers profusely in the summer.

Geranium 'Johnson's Blue'

Spreads in a loose mound by underground rhizomatous roots. The leaves are intermediate between *G. pratense* and *G. himalayense*. They are medium green, with seven lobes, narrow divisions, and a faint gray tinge. They are deeply divided and toothed. Many gardeners admire this plant for its large, abundant light blue flowers whose petals are spoon shaped and have translucent veins.

ZONES 5–9
PLANT SIZE 18 × 36 in. (45 × 90 cm)
SOIL Moderately moist loam, mildly acidic to neutral to alkaline
LIGHT Full sun in mild summer gardens, morning sun and afternoon shade in hot summer gardens
PROPAGATION Crown division, roots
ORIGIN *G. pratense* × *G. himalayense*. It was raised from seed of *G. pratense*, which A. T. Johnson of Wales sent to B. Ruys of Dedemsvaart, Netherlands, around 1950.
GARDEN AND DESIGN USES Perennial borders, containers, over a wall
NOTES If there was one geranium that gardeners had heard of before the advent of *G.* 'Rozanne', it was *G.* 'Johnson's Blue'. This is an undeniably lovely plant, but it does not grow well for everyone. In a hot summer garden, 'Johnson's Blue' is likely to disappear in a couple of years. It grows well in coolish summers. Although the plant is sterile, there is another cross, probably using the same parentage, available in the United States and distributed under the same name. The imposter's leaves more closely resemble *G. pratense* and the flowers are a deeper blue with bright reddish veins. The flowers have blunt ends to the petals. It is taller and less compact than 'Johnson's Blue', and is fertile.

Geranium 'Joy'

Satisfying and easy to grow. The five- to seven-lobed leaves are faintly marbled and form an attractive mound. The flowers are bowl shaped, 1¼ inches (3.1 cm), and pale pink with magenta veins.

ZONES 8–9
PLANT SIZE 12–15 × 18 in. (30–38 × 45 cm)
SOIL Moderately moist loam, mildly acidic to neutral
LIGHT Morning sun in mild summer gardens
PROPAGATION Crown division
ORIGIN *G. traversii* var. *elegans* × *G. lambertii*. In 1992, Alan Bremner hybridized this and Axletree Nursery, United Kingdom, distributed it. The plant was named after Joy Jones, one of the authors of *The Gardeners Guide to Growing Hardy Geraniums*. *Geranium* 'Joy' resembles its parent *G. traversii* var. *elegans* in that it doesn't like winter temperatures below 25°F (−3.9°C).
GARDEN AND DESIGN USES Front of a perennial border, containers
NOTES Although it is not particularly floriferous, the combination of marbled leaves and delicate pink flowers makes it an attractive addition to the front of a perennial border.

Geranium '**Karen Wouters**'

Large mounding clump with yellow-green leaves that are pebbled and deeply veined, with five broad lobes. Medium lavender flowers veined dark purple. Petals are separated and notched.

ZONES 5–10

PLANT SIZE 18–20 × 20 in. (40–45 × 50 cm)

SOIL Moderately fertile loam, well-drained, neutral to slightly alkaline

LIGHT Morning sun and afternoon shade

PROPAGATION Crown division

ORIGIN A seedling from G. 'Chantilly'. Found by Mia Esser in her garden and named for Karen Wouters, Wouters Vaste Planten, Netherlands.

GARDEN AND DESIGN USES Perennial border, containers

Geranium 'Kashmir Blue'◂

It has upright growth, similar to *G. pratense*. Leaves are narrowly lobed and finely dissected with five to seven wedge-shaped lobes that are deeply divided and somewhat overlapping. The flowers are large, pale soft blue with separated petals.

ZONES 5–9
PLANT SIZE 18 × 18 in. (45 × 45 cm)
SOIL Light loam, slightly acidic to neutral
LIGHT Morning sun and afternoon shade
PROPAGATION Crown division
ORIGIN *G. pratense* f. *albiflorum* × *G. clarkei* 'Kashmir White'. From De Bloemenhoek Nursery, Netherlands, in 1990. Ivan Louette, Belgium, raised it in the mid-1980s.
GARDEN AND DESIGN USES Perennial borders
NOTES If you cut back the plant after flowering, it will regrow and reflower. It flowers in late spring through early summer.

Geranium 'Kashmir Pink'▴

Mounds of medium green narrowly lobed leaves and soft pink flowers with purple veins.

ZONES 5–9
PLANT SIZE 15 × 18 in. (38 × 45 cm)
SOIL Light well-drained loam, neutral to alkaline
LIGHT Full sun in mild coastal gardens, morning sun and afternoon shade in hot summer gardens. 'Kashmir Pink' is more sun tolerant than the color forms of *G. clarkei*, namely 'Kashmir Purple' and 'Kashmir White'.
PROPAGATION Crown division
ORIGIN A seedling from *G. clarkei* 'Kashmir Purple'. From Blackthorn Nursery, United Kingdom, in 1990, and raised by Robin White.
GARDEN AND DESIGN USES Perennial borders, containers
NOTES Flowers in spring through early summer.

Geranium 'Kirsty' ▲

A large spreading plant with leaves that are deeply divided and narrowly lobed. The big white cup-shaped flowers have purple veins and face upward.

ZONES 5–9
PLANT SIZE 20 × 24 in. (50 × 60 cm)
SOIL Moderately fertile loam, well-drained, slightly acidic to neutral
LIGHT Morning sun and afternoon shade
PROPAGATION Crown division
ORIGIN *G. clarkei* 'Kashmir White' × *G. regelii*. Alan Bremner raised it, and Judith Bradshaw of Catforth Gardens, United Kingdom, named it after her granddaughter.
GARDEN AND DESIGN USES Perennial borders, containers
NOTES The flowers are very attractive, and it is a great addition to a perennial border.

Geranium kishtvariense ▲

Forms a loose spreading mound with long flowering stems. It has rhizomatous, creeping roots and dark green five-lobed, wrinkled leaves in three to five serrated divisions. The leaves have swollen nodes and leaf stalk bases. The flowers are 1½ inches (3.8 cm) wide and deep pink with a white star-shaped center and dark reddish purple veins.

ZONES 7–9
PLANT SIZE 10 × 24–30 in. (25 × 60–75 cm)
SOIL Moderately damp loam, mildly acidic to neutral
LIGHT Light shade
PROPAGATION Crown division, seed
ORIGIN From Kashmir. Roy Lancaster originally collected it in 1978 from a forest location.
GARDEN AND DESIGN USES Front of a perennial border, over a wall, containers
NOTES Looks quite similar to *G. rubifolium*, but the rhizomatous roots occur only in *G. kishtvariense*. The plant is slow growing, so locate it carefully at the front of the perennial border so its neighbors will not engulf it.

Geranium koreanum ▾

Forms a spreading mound of deep green five-lobed, marbled leaves on long, thin stems from a short rhizomatous root. It has rose-pink upward-facing flowers with a pale eye and violet veins.

ZONES 5–9
PLANT SIZE 15 × 24 in. (38 × 60 cm)
SOIL Moderately fertile loam, well-drained, slightly acidic to neutral
LIGHT Morning sun to light shade
PROPAGATION Seed
ORIGIN From Chirisan Mountain, Korea, in forest clearings and mountain woods near streams.
GARDEN AND DESIGN USES Perennial borders in morning sun, light shade borders
NOTES Similar to *G. koreanum*, and the two plants are hard for gardeners to distinguish.

Geranium krameri

Medium green five-lobed, deeply dissected leaves and long flowering stems. The flowers are pale pink with deeper lavender-pink veins.

ZONES 5–9
PLANT SIZE 10 × 36 in. (25 × 90 cm)
SOIL Moderately moist, well-drained loam, neutral to mildly acidic
LIGHT Light shade
PROPAGATION Crown division, seed
ORIGIN Northern China (south to west Hubei), the Far Eastern Russian Federation, Korea, and Japan
GARDEN AND DESIGN USES Low areas in front of a shade garden
NOTES Needs summer water and partial shade to grow well.

Geranium 'Lilac Ice'

Forms a fairly compact mound and is self branching. It has the same light green leaves as G. 'Rozanne' but with paler blotches. It bears 2¼-inch (5.7 cm) pale ice-blue flowers with darker veins. It is a sport of 'Rozanne' but does not have the prominent color ring on the petals. It flowers from summer to fall. It is not as floriferous as 'Rozanne', but the color of the flowers makes it very unusual.

ZONES 5–10

PLANT SIZE 15 × 24 in. (38 × 60 cm)

SOIL Medium loam, slightly acidic to neutral to slightly acidic. Moderate water. Will tolerate some drought when established.

LIGHT Full sun in mild summer gardens, morning sun and afternoon shade in hot summer gardens

PROPAGATION Restricted to licensed propagators

ORIGIN Michael and Thomas Waterer selected it from a large group of G. 'Rozanne', and it was patented in 2008.

GARDEN AND DESIGN USES Perennial border, containers

Geranium 'Little Gem' ▾

A low-growing mound of gray-green leaves with five broad, deeply divided lobes. The flowers are light magenta with a small white eye.

ZONES 8–10
PLANT SIZE 10 × 18 in. (25 × 45 cm)
SOIL Moderately moist and well-drained loam, slightly acidic to neutral to slightly alkaline
LIGHT Full sun in mild summer gardens
PROPAGATION Crown division
ORIGIN *G.* ×*oxonianum* × *G. traversii*. Alan Bremner, Orkney Islands, United Kingdom, raised it in 1990. The flowers and the plant are smaller than *G.* ×*riversleaianum* 'Russell Prichard'.
GARDEN AND DESIGN USES Front of a perennial border, containers

Geranium ×magnificum ◄

Makes a large and spreading mound. The medium green leaves are large, hairy, overlapping, nine- to eleven-lobed, and toothed. The flowers are deep purple with dark purple veins.

ZONES 5–10

PLANT SIZE 24–30 × 36 in. (60–75 × 90 cm)

SOIL Moderately moist loam, slightly acidic to neutral; will tolerate some dryness when established

LIGHT Full sun in mild summer gardens, morning sun and afternoon shade in hot summer gardens

PROPAGATION Crown division

ORIGIN Possibly *G. platypetalum* × *G. ibericum* subsp. *ibericum*. It has been in cultivation since before 1961.

GARDEN AND DESIGN USES Perennial borders, shrub borders

NOTES This old, well-established geranium in perennial borders makes a vigorous spreading mound. It is sterile. The flowering period is somewhat short, from early to late spring. It remains an attractive mound of leaves for the rest of the growing season. It is very tolerant of high summer heat.

CULTIVARS

G. ×*magnificum* **'Ernst Pagels'** 20 × 24 in. (50 × 60 cm). This comes from the garden of Coen Jansen in Netherlands and was named after a well-known Dutch nurseryman. It is thought to come from *G.* ×*magnificum* 'Peter Yeo', even though that plant was believed to be sterile. The plant has basal leaves that do not overlap much. Its flowers are violet.

G. ×*magnificum* **'Hylander'** 18 × 24 in. (45 × 60 cm). From Richard Clifton in 1979. This is the name given to the original Clone A of Peter Yeo's *Hardy Geraniums*. It is named after Nils Hylander, the botanist who first described *G.* ×*magnificum* in 1961. The flowers are dark blue-purple.

G. ×*magnificum* **'Peter Yeo'** ▲ 20 × 24 in. (50 × 60 cm). From Richard Clifton, 1979. This is the name given to the original Clone C of Peter Yeo's *Hardy Geraniums*. It grows large violet-blue flowers with dark purple veins and wide, overlapping petals.

G. ×*magnificum* **'Rosemoor'** 20 × 24 in. (50 × 60 cm). A more compact, repeat flowering clone from the Hans Simon nursery, Germany, in 1997. Named after the garden Rosemoor in the United Kingdom. The flowers are a lighter red-violet than *G.* ×*magnificum*.

Geranium 'Mavis Simpson'◂

A large, mounding, gray-leafed plant with long flowering stems. Flowers are 1¼ inches (3.1 cm) wide and pale pink with pink veins and a white center. Flowering is prolific.

ZONES 8–10

PLANT SIZE 18 × 36–48 in. (45 × 90–122 cm)

SOIL Moderately moist loam, sandy soil or amended clay with good drainage, mildly acidic to neutral

LIGHT Full sun in mild summer gardens, morning sun and afternoon shade in hot summer gardens

PROPAGATION Crown division

ORIGIN A chance seedling from The Royal Botanic Garden, Kew, United Kingdom. Mr. Cook, Royal Botanic Garden supervisor, found this prior to 1982, and named it after a member of the Alpine Garden staff.

GARDEN AND DESIGN USES Perennial borders, garden walls, containers. The flowering stems will trail through other perennials.

NOTES Very similar to another seedling, G. 'Jean Armour', but the former has no veins on the back of the petals. Cut back flowering stems to the crown, as they become untidy as the growing season progresses. New stems and new flowers will appear.

Geranium 'Maxwelton'▾

Forms a large mound with big pale green leaves that have three to five broad, deep lobes. The foliage turns yellow in autumn. The plant has cupped light-magenta flowers with a small dark eye and fine black to dark pink veins radiating out from the center.

ZONES 5–9

PLANT SIZE 36 × 36 in. (90 × 90 cm)

SOIL Well amended, moderately moist loam, well-drained, mildly acidic to neutral

LIGHT Full sun in mild summer gardens, morning sun and afternoon shade in hot summer gardens

PROPAGATION Crown division, roots

ORIGIN G. psilostemon × G. ×oxonianum 'Wargrave Pink'. From John Ross, Charter House Nursery, Scotland, in 1985.

GARDEN AND DESIGN USES Perennial border, large containers

Geranium 'Mrs. Jean Moss'. ▲

Light green leaves with broad divisions and notable veining. Strong and tall flowering stems produce purple-pink flowers without a white eye, with light purple veins.

ZONES 5–9
PLANT SIZE 24 × 24 in. (60 × 60 cm)
SOIL Moderately damp and fertile loam, slightly acidic to neutral
LIGHT Morning sun to light shade; no hot afternoon sun
PROPAGATION Crown division
ORIGIN A seedling of G. 'Tidmarsh'. Robin Moss named this for his wife, and The Plantsman's Preference first published it in 2008.
GARDEN DESIGN AND USES Shade garden
NOTES Looks somewhat similar to G. *sylvaticum*.

Geranium 'Nimbus'

Forms a mound of seven-lobed, finely dissected, and sharply toothed leaves that have a yellow cast when they emerge in spring. The leaves turn medium green in summer. The flowers are a blue-lavender with purple-magenta veins and a small pale zone at the base, and they are about 1 inch (2.5 cm) in diameter. The petals are separated from each other.

ZONES 5–9
PLANT SIZE 24 × 36 in. (60 × 90 cm)
SOIL Moderately moist loam, neutral to mildly acidic
LIGHT Full sun in mild summer gardens, morning sun and afternoon shade in hot summer gardens
PROPAGATION Crown division
ORIGIN *G. clarkei* 'Kashmir Purple' × *G. collinum*. Found on the research plots of Cambridge University Botanic Garden in 1979. Axletree Nursery, United Kingdom, distributed it in 1990.
GARDEN AND DESIGN USES Perennial borders, containers
NOTES Highly floriferous and flowers for a long period of time. It benefits from growing through other plants for support.

Geranium 'Nunwood Purple'

A mound of medium green rounded, deeply lobed leaves. It has blue-purple flowers with a red flush toward the center of the flower and overlapping petals.

ZONES 5–9
PLANT SIZE 12 × 18 in. (30 × 45 cm)
SOIL Moderately fertile loam, slightly damp, slightly acidic to neutral
LIGHT Full sun in mild summer gardens, morning sun and afternoon shade in hot summer gardens
PROPAGATION Crown division
ORIGIN *G. pratense* f. *albiflorum* × *G. himalayense* 'Gravetye'. John Ross, Charter House Nursery, Scotland, released it in 1989.
GARDEN AND DESIGN USES Front of the perennial border, in a shrub border in morning sun
NOTES Cut back after flowering for repeat bloom.

Geranium 'Orion'

A tall clumping perennial, with leaves that resemble *G. pratense*. The lobes are narrow and deeply dissected. It has lavender-blue large, saucer-shaped flowers, 2¼ inches (5.7 cm) in diameter, with a small white eye. It blooms in the spring and summer.

ZONES 5–9

PLANT SIZE 24–30 × 24–36 in. (60–75 × 60–90 cm)

SOIL Moderately damp loam, well-drained, slightly acidic to neutral

LIGHT Full sun in mild summer gardens, morning sun and afternoon shade in hot summers

PROPAGATION Crown division

ORIGIN Possibly *G*. 'Brookside' × *G. ibericum*. A sterile hybrid from *G*. 'Brookside', which Brian Kabbes found in the Netherlands.

GARDEN AND DESIGN USES Mid border plant in a perennial border and a ground cover under lightly shaded shrubs and trees.

NOTES When initially planted, it will need support for the first couple of seasons until clumps increase in size and become more self supporting. A horticultural corset of adjacent shrubs or tall perennials will obviate the need for staking. If it gets untidy, cut back to the crown. It will regrow and reflower in the late summer. Good fall color has been reported in cold climates.

HYBRIDS

G. 'Eureka Blue'

Geranium 'Orkney Blue'▾

A mound of medium green rounded, deeply lobed leaves that have five to seven slightly overlapping lobes with toothed margins. The plant appears to be intermediate between its two parents. It has dark blue-purple heavily veined flowers 1½ inches (3.8 cm) in diameter.

ZONES 5–9
PLANT SIZE 20 × 18 in. (50 × 45 cm)
SOIL Moderately moist loam, well-drained, slightly acidic to neutral soil
LIGHT Morning sun only; can take afternoon shade
PROPAGATION Crown division
ORIGIN *G. ibericum* subsp. *jubatum* × *G. gymnocaulon*. An Alan Bremner hybrid, published in 2003 by Crûg Farm Plants, Wales.
GARDEN AND DESIGN USES Perennial borders, containers
NOTES Flowers in spring.

Geranium 'Orkney Dawn'▸

A neat mound of leaves that are pebbled and veined like *G. renardii*. They emerge in the spring as bright yellow, later changing to pale yellow-green in the summer. It has lavender-blue flowers with dark, almost black veins. The petals are notched and separated. The flowers are produced over many weeks on 16-inch (40 cm) stems that are held well above the contrasting wrinkled leaves.

ZONES 5–9
PLANT SIZE 16 × 18 in. (40 × 45 cm)
SOIL Moderately moist, well-drained loam, slightly acidic to neutral
LIGHT Morning sun only
PROPAGATION Crown division
ORIGIN *G. peloponnesiacum* × *G. renardii*. An Alan Bremner hybrid from Crûg Farm Plants, Wales, in 2003.
GARDEN AND DESIGN USES Perennial border, containers
NOTES Flowers in midspring to early summer.

Geranium palustre ▸

A bushy plant with light green basal leaves that are five-lobed and sharply dissected. It has magenta-pink flowers with a small white center, 1½ inches (3.8 cm) in diameter.

ZONES 5–9
PLANT SIZE 15–18 × 24 in. (38–45 × 60 cm)
SOIL It likes damp, fertile loam, but it will also tolerate somewhat dry soil, mildly acidic to neutral.
LIGHT Morning sun; the leaves tend to burn in hot summer afternoon sun
PROPAGATION Crown division, seed
ORIGIN Eastern and central Europe up into northern Europe; damp meadows, ditches, forest edges
GARDEN AND DESIGN USES Useful for a dampish place in a perennial border and in areas of heavy irrigation. The flowering period is fairly short, about a month in the middle of summer, but it is such an attractive sight it deserves a place in the garden.

Geranium 'Patricia'

A large mound of light green leaves with five to seven lobes that become red-flecked with age. The foliage turns bronze in fall. Flowers are red-purple with darker veins and a dark, shiny center.

ZONES 3–9
PLANT SIZE 24–36 × 36 in. (60–90 × 90 cm)
SOIL Well amended, moderately moist loam, mildly acidic to neutral to mildly alkaline
LIGHT Full sun in mild summer gardens, morning sun and afternoon shade in hot summer gardens
PROPAGATION Crown division
ORIGIN *G. endressii* × *G. psilostemon*. Alan Bremner named it after Patricia Doughty, Orkney Islands, United Kingdom, in 1992.
GARDEN AND DESIGN USES Perennial borders, containers
NOTES The plant is sterile. Cut back hard after flowering to produce new leaves and flowers.

Geranium peloponnesiacum

Forms a mound of quilted leaves in the spring that come from thick rhizomatous roots. The leaves have three to five diamond-shaped, irregularly toothed lobes. The flowering stems are around 24 inches (60 cm) long and are held well above the leaves. The flowers are pale violet-blue, 1½ inches (3.8 cm) across, with notched petals and violet veins. It blooms in spring and can go dormant in summer.

ZONES 5–9
PLANT SIZE 15–18 × 20 in. (38–45 × 50 cm)
SOIL Light loam, moderate water, neutral and possibly slightly acidic or slightly alkaline
LIGHT Full sun in mild summer gardens, morning sun and afternoon shade in hot summer gardens
PROPAGATION Division of rhizomes, seed
ORIGIN Albania and southern Greece, found in shaded areas. It was collected in the Pindus mountains. Richard Gorer introduced this into gardens in the United Kingdom in 1972.
GARDEN AND DESIGN USES Perennial borders, containers
HYBRIDS
G. 'Stephanie' ▶ Parentage possibly *G. peloponnesiacum* × *G. renardii*. 12 × 15 in. (30 × 38 cm). It is a smaller, quite compact, mounding version of *G. peloponnesiacum*. It was an accidental seedling from the Royal Botanic Garden Edinburgh. It is useful for the edge of the border or a rock garden. Flowers are lavender-blue with dark purple veins, 1½ inches (3.8 cm) in diameter.

Geranium 'Philippe Vapelle'

It has seven-lobed leaves with a pebbled surface similar to one of its parents, *G. renardii*. The flowers are light lavender-blue with purple veins and the petals are deeply notched and separated.

ZONES 5–10
PLANT SIZE 15–18 × 24 in. (38–45 × 60 cm)
SOIL Moderately damp, fertile loam, but will also grow in amended clay, rocky and sandy soil. Will withstand some drought. Neutral to mildly acidic.
LIGHT Morning sun
PROPAGATION Crown division
ORIGIN *G. platypetalum* × *G. renardii*. Ivan Louette, Belgium, raised the plant and named it after a friend. Alan Bremner hybridized an almost identical plant, which Axletree Nursery, United Kingdom, distributed in 1991 under the same name.
GARDEN AND DESIGN USES Front of perennial borders, containers, rock gardens
NOTES A handsome plant for the front of a perennial border. Its flowering period is comparatively short, although it will sometimes reflower. It tolerates heat in hot summers if you grow it in light shade.

Geranium platyanthum ▶

It makes tall upright mounds with large, hairy, toothed leaves divided into five to seven broad lobes. It has 1- to 1½-inch (2.5–3.8 cm) flowers that are flat, disc shaped, then reflexed as they age, in dense clusters on tall stems. They are mauve-blue, fading to a white center.

ZONES 5–9
PLANT SIZE 18 × 24 in. (45 × 60 cm)
SOIL Moderate loam, well-drained, neutral to mildly acidic
LIGHT Morning sun to light shade
PROPAGATION Crown division, seed
ORIGIN Siberia, eastern Tibet, western China, Korea, and Japan
GARDEN AND DESIGN USES Perennial border, shrub border, wild garden. Plants will tolerate dry shade, although they look better with light summer watering.
NOTES The flowers look small in proportion to the leaves and the blooming time is brief, but the plant makes a handsome accent mound of leaves. There is good fall color.
CULTIVARS
G. platyanthum **'Ankum'** 18 × 24 in. (45 × 60 cm). Chosen by Coen Jansen, Vaste Plante, Netherlands, with white flowers.
G. platyanthum **'Russian Giant'** 30 × 24 in. (75 × 60 cm). The Plantsman's Preference, United Kingdom, published this purple-flowered, very strongly growing form in 2005.

Geranium platypetalum

Hairy, rounded, seven- to nine-lobed leaves that are slightly pebbled and divided to about half of their depth. The divisions are broadly lobed and toothed. The flowers are dark blue-violet with violet veins.

ZONES 5–10

PLANT SIZE 15–18 × 18 in. (38–45 × 45 cm)

SOIL Moderately fertile loam, well-drained, mildly acidic to neutral

LIGHT Full sun in mild summer gardens, morning sun and afternoon shade in hot summer gardens

PROPAGATION Crown division

ORIGIN From northeast Turkey and northwest Iran. In Turkey it grows in woody and scrubby areas.

GARDEN AND DESIGN USES Perennial borders, containers

NOTES Provides a much more compact and tidy appearance than G. ibericum, and is very useful for a perennial border.

CULTIVARS

G. platypetalum **'Genyell'** 18 × 24 in. (45 × 60 cm). From Cherry Tree Lodge, United Kingdom, in 2002. Possibly the same plant as *G. platypetalum* 'Turco'. If so, 'Turco' has precedence.

G. platypetalum **'Georgia Blue'** ▲ 15 × 18 in. (38 × 45 cm). Roy Lancaster collected this in 1979 in Klukorsky Pass, Sochumi, Caucasus. Flowers are deep blue-violet, saucer shaped, violet veined, and 1½ inches (3.8 cm) in diameter. It is the most attractive, longest-flowering of these selections.

G. platypetalum **'Turco'** 15 × 18 in. (38 × 45 cm). From Rolf Offenthal, Germany, 1996, and reportedly collected in eastern Turkey. It has large violet-blue flowers with a white eye and deep violet veins. It looks very similar to 'Genyell', and may be the same plant.

HYBRIDS

G. ×magnificum

G. 'Philippe Vapelle'

Geranium pratense (Double Forms)

Large mounds of finely dissected medium green leaves with seven to nine lobes. All the plants listed here have double flowers in white, lavender, or violet. They flower in late spring to midsummer.

ZONES 3–9

PLANT SIZE 12–24 × 15–20 in. (30–60 × 38–50 cm)

SOIL Loam, moderate water, slightly acidic to neutral to slightly alkaline

LIGHT Full sun in mild summer gardens. All forms of *G. pratense* grow better in mild summer gardens.

PROPAGATION Crown division

ORIGIN *G. pratense* 'Plenum Violaceum' has been known since the 16th century. *G. pratense* 'Laura' appeared in a packet of *G. pratense* 'Album' seed.

GARDEN AND DESIGN USES Perennial borders, containers

NOTES There is a tendency for all forms of *G. pratense* to develop powdery and downy mildew during midsummer through the fall. Providing good air circulation and allowing irrigation water to dry off the leaves before nightfall helps keep the mildew at bay. Cutting diseased plants back to the crown and carefully disposing of the infected parts also helps. The double forms appear to be sterile, although *G. pratense* 'Laura' appeared from a batch of seed.

CULTIVARS

***G. pratense* 'Plenum Album'** 20 × 18 in. (50 × 45 cm). Walter Ingwersen published this very old cultivar in 1946 as "var. *album flore plenum*." Some stock are diseased and dwindle away. This plant is difficult to maintain in the garden.

G. pratense 'Double Jewel' ◀ 12 × 15 in. (30 × 38 cm). A. Verschoor Horticulture, Netherlands, introduced this into horticulture. It is a dwarf form of *G. pratense* that has white double flowers with petalloid stamens veined red-pink in the center.

G. pratense 'Laura' ▶ 20 × 18 in. (50 × 45 cm). This appeared in Christine Morley's garden in Cheshire, United Kingdom, after a packet of mixed *G. pratense* seed was sown, and is named for her mother. It produces beautifully formed rosebud-shaped flowers in white and has mounds of medium green narrowly lobed leaves. 'Laura' is sturdy and healthy, but subject to powdery and downy mildew in late summer, as are many of the forms of *G. pratense*. Site it carefully in an open location.

G. pratense 'Plenum Caeruleum' 20 × 18 in. (50 × 45 cm). Walter Ingwersen published this very old cultivar in 1946 as "var. *caerulea flore plenum*." Light lavender-blue flowers have a small, darker lavender center, about 1¼ inches (3.1 cm) in diameter. Not such a perfect rosette as 'Plenum Violaceum'.

G. pratense 'Plenum Violaceum' ◀ 24 × 20 in. (60 × 50 cm). Another very old cultivar, originally described as "var. *violacea flore plenum*" by Walter Ingwersen, United Kingdom, in 1946. Double violet flowers in a perfect rosebud shape that become red-purple in the center.

G. pratense 'Summer Skies' 20 × 18 in. (50 × 45 cm). From Kevin Nicholson, United Kingdom, via Blooms of Bressingham. Finely cut green foliage and small clusters of double flowers in light lavender with a white center. Restricted to licensed propagators.

Geranium pratense (Single Flowers)

Tall, with finely cut leaves making an imposing mound, five to nine lobes with long, pointed, irregular teeth. Tall flowering stems arise from the mound. The roots are thick, finger-like, and quite long, and plants respond to deep, fertile soil. The flowers are saucer shaped, 1¼ to 1½ inches (3.1–3.8 cm), and are white or all shades of blue and pink.

ZONES 3–9

PLANT SIZE 18 × 36 in. (45 × 90 cm)

SOIL Medium loam, well-drained, slightly acidic to neutral to alkaline. Many single-flowered forms grow very well in alkaline soil.

LIGHT Full sun in mild summer gardens. Afternoon shade is required in hot summer gardens, but plants may also struggle in high summer heat.

PROPAGATION Seed for species, crown division for named cultivars

ORIGIN The wild forms of *G. pratense* have an enormous range throughout Europe and central Asia to the Himalayas, Nepal, Kashmir, and Pakistan. They have naturalized in the top third of the eastern and central United States. There are morphological differences between plants in the various locales, but for garden purposes, the culture is similar. There are more than 45 named forms of *G. pratense* in *The Plant Finder*.

GARDEN AND DESIGN USES Perennial borders, containers, meadow gardens

NOTES Powdery and downy mildew in the summer are the main problems. Locate plants in areas with good air circulation and morning sun, and water during the day so the leaves will dry before evening. This will help mitigate, but not prevent, the onset of powdery and downy mildews.

VARIETIES

G. pratense var. *stewartianum* 'Elizabeth Yeo' 24 × 30 in. (60 × 75 cm). Peter Yeo selected this and named it for his wife. It has dusky medium pink flowers and coarsely but deeply dissected leaves. There is a second form, 'Raina', with dark veins on the petals, but it does not appear to be available in the United States.

FORMS

G. pratense* f. *albiflorum ▲ 18–20 × 24 in. (45–50 × 60 cm). A white-flowered form of the species collected in the wild. Flowers are variable in petal size and shape. The best selections are sturdy and heavy flowering.

CULTIVARS

***G. pratense* 'Bittersweet'** 18 × 18 in. (45 × 45 cm). A very pale pink-blue form from Monksilver Nursery, United Kingdom, 1990.

***G. pratense* 'Black Beauty'** 18 × 24 in. (45 × 60 cm). Selected by Nori Pope, Hadspen Garden, in 2002. It is the best maroon-leaf selection of *G. pratense* 'Victor Reiter', but it is unaccountably difficult to find in nurseries. Unlike *G. pratense* 'Midnight Reiter', it grows strongly. Medium blue flowers.

***G. pratense* 'Cielito Lindo'** ▲ 18 × 24 in. (45 × 60 cm). From Geraniaceae Nursery, California, in 1997. Its flowers are light blue.

***G. pratense* 'Cluden Sapphire'** 20 × 24 in. (50 × 60 cm). From Charter House Nursery, United Kingdom, in 1992. John Ross collected it from Cluden Water, Dumfries. The flowers are brilliant blue.

***G. pratense* 'Galactic'** (see photo on page 32) 18 × 24 in. (45 × 60 cm). A beautiful cultivated form of the white *G. pratense* with overlapping white petals.

***G. pratense* 'Hocus Pocus'** 18 × 24 in. (45 × 60 cm). From Claire Austin Hardy Plants in 2003. One of a number of brown-maroon leaf selections of *G. pratense* 'Victor Reiter'. Flowers are lavender-purple.

***G. pratense* 'Ilja'** 24 × 24 in. (60 × 60 cm). This is a wonderful selection with large white flowers and purple veins. The flowers were originally described as lilac-pink with darker pink veining, so this may be a case of mistaken identity.

***G. pratense* 'Midnight Blues'** 14 × 15 in. (36 × 38 cm). From Thierry Delabroye in France, this is possibly a sport of *G. pratense* 'Midnight Reiter' with deeper black-purple glossy foliage. It has light blue flowers with rose veins, and the blooms are held well above the leaves.

***G. pratense* 'Midnight Clouds'** 15 × 18 in. (38 × 45 cm). Luc Klinkhamer found this in the Netherlands. It forms a compact, neat clump with finely dissected maroon to maroon-green leaves. The plant requires morning sun and afternoon shade in all but the mildest

summer gardens. It is not prone to powdery mildew, which affects so many forms of *G. pratense*. The flowers are white with dark veins, and it blooms from late spring through summer. A useful plant for the front of a perennial border.

***G. pratense* 'Midnight Reiter'** 10–12 × 15 in. (25–30 × 38 cm). Dan Hinkley of Bainbridge Island, Washington, selected and named this, and it was published by Axletree Nursery, United Kingdom, in 2003. This seed selection from *G. pratense* 'Victor Reiter' has deep maroon-red leaves, and growth is compact and slow. The flowers are dark violet-blue.

***G. pratense* 'Milk Cow Blues'** 18 × 24 in. (45 × 60 cm). From Robin Moss, United Kingdom. Its flowers are a pale, almost translucent blue.

***G. pratense* 'Mrs. Kendall Clark'** 18–20 × 24 in. (45–50 × 60 cm). The flowers are pale violet-blue with white veins. This is not the color as originally described before 1946, but this plant has usurped the original, according to Peter Yeo, and is now widely distributed.

***G. pratense* 'New Dimension'** ▲ 20 × 24 in. (50 × 60 cm). Discovered in Vinhega, Netherlands, as a mutation from *G. pratense* 'Victor Reiter' and patented in 2003. The flowers are a light violet-blue. The leaves are green with a maroon-brown stain that deepens in the sun.

***G. pratense* 'Purple Ghost'** 12–15 × 15 in. (30–38 × 38 cm). A form of *G. pratense* 'Black Beauty'. New World Plants, United Kingdom, introduced this, and it was distributed in 2015. Flowers have a palest lavender to almost white background with an intricate tracery of light purple veins.

***G. pratense* 'Silver Queen'** ◀ 24 × 24 in. (60 × 60 cm). A. T. Johnson, United Kingdom, originally raised this in 1926 and described it as having silver-blue flowers. The plant currently grown under the name has very pale gray-blue flowers that are almost white, with sooty black anthers.

G. pratense '**Striatum**' ◄ 24 × 30 in. (60 × 75 cm). Commercially known as 'Splish-Splash', this has white flowers that are irregularly streaked and spotted in pale and dark blue. Sometimes flowers are all blue, and sometimes all white. Its name has a long and confused history.

G. pratense '**Victor Reiter**' ▲ 18 × 24 in. (45 × 60 cm). Victor Reiter grew this in his garden in San Francisco in the 1980s and distributed it. Seedlings are quite variable, as is plant size. A number of named cultivars have arisen from this plant, which has green-maroon leaves and medium blue flowers.

G. pratense '**Wisley Blue**' 18 × 24–30 in. (45 × 60–90 cm). From Rosie's Garden Plants, United Kingdom, in 1998. Originally from The Royal Horticultural Society at Wisley and reintroduced by Croftway Nursery, United Kingdom, in 1988. It has medium blue flowers with red veins.

G. pratense **'Yorkshire Queen'** ▲ 18 × 24 in. (45 × 60 cm). White flowers with purple veins. Found by Robin Moss and published by Axletree Nursery, United Kingdom, in 1995.

HYBRIDS Alan Bremner has crossed *G. collinum* with all the *G. pratense* forms available.

G. **'Distant Hills'** ▶ Parentage *G. pratense* × *G. collinum*. 30 × 36 in. (75 × 90 cm). Alan Bremner raised this, and Charter House Nursery, United Kingdom, published it in 1994. Flowers are misty blue with purple veins, about 1½ inches (3.1 cm) wide, and the petals are spoon shaped.

G. **'Eva'**

Geranium 'Prelude'

Makes a dense mound of soft medium green leaves that have five to seven slightly overlapping lobes with toothed margins. The leaves resemble *G. albiflorum*. It has clusters of small lavender blue flowers with magenta veins in the spring.

ZONES 5–9
PLANT SIZE 12–18 × 24 in. (30–45 × 60 cm)
SOIL Moderately damp loam, reasonably fertile, slightly acidic to neutral
LIGHT Light shade
PROPAGATION Crown division
ORIGIN *G. albiflorum* × *G. sylvaticum*. An Alan Bremner hybrid from Catforth Gardens, United Kingdom, in 1994.
GARDEN AND DESIGN USES A shade garden or a light shade shrub border, perhaps mixed in with spring bulbs
NOTES Flowers early in the summer. Cut back hard after flowering and it will make a mound of new leaves, but no new flowers.

Geranium psilostemon

Very large, deeply divided, seven-lobed, and acutely toothed leaves that form basal clumps up to 36 inches (90 cm) wide. The flowers are a very strong magenta with a black eye and black veins.

ZONES 5–9
PLANT SIZE 36 × 36 in. (90 × 90 cm)
SOIL Excellent quality loam, rich and fertile, neutral to slightly acidic
LIGHT Full sun in mild summer gardens
PROPAGATION Seed for species, crown division for cultivars
ORIGIN Valleys in northeastern Turkey, southwestern Caucasus. It was introduced into cultivation in the United Kingdom in 1874.
GARDEN AND DESIGN USES Perennial border, large containers
NOTES Flowers occur on tall branched stems that can flop down when the plant is young, although as the basal clumps age they become somewhat more self supporting. Leave sufficient space for this plant in the back of a perennial border. It appears to resent disturbance, so site it where it will grow permanently. It is one of the few geraniums that requires vegetable garden–quality soil. It performs poorly in climates with extreme summer heat and humidity.

CULTIVARS

G. psilostemon **'Bressingham Flair'** 36 × 36 in. (90 × 90 cm). Alan Bloom raised this in the mid-1960s. It has a similar habit to *G. psilostemon*, but the flowers are a pale milky magenta with maroon veins and a maroon basal blotch.

G. psilostemon **'Coton Goliath'** 72 × 36 in. (180 × 90 cm). From Betty Ellis, Coton, Cambridge, United Kingdom, and published by The Plantsman's Preference in 2004–2005. The flowers are magenta and normal size. This engaging monster needs careful siting in the garden.

G. psilostemon **'Jason Bloom'** 46 × 36 in. (120 × 90 cm). Introduced by Bressingham Gardens, United Kingdom, around 2010. It has 2- to 2½-inch (5–6 cm) magenta flowers that are held well above the leaves. Flowering is profuse.

HYBRIDS

G. **'Catherine Deneuve'** Parentage possibly *G. psilostemon* × *G.* ×*oxonianum* f. *thurstonianum*. 18 × 36 in. (45 × 90 cm). Discovered in Hantay, France, in 2009, and introduced by Sandrine Delabroye, Netherlands. The plant is upright and spreads broadly, and has medium green leaves with three to five acute lobes. The flowers are star shaped with very narrow petals that are pointed or notched, and are carmine with dark red veins. They are 1¾ inches (4.4 cm) in diameter.

G. **'Little David'** Parentage *G. psilostemon* × *G. sanguineum* 'Droplet'. 6–8 × 12 in. (15–20 × 30 cm). Alan Bremner raised this and Axletree Nursery, United Kingdom, published it in 1996. It has a compact form, strong magenta flowers, and the robust habit of *G. sanguineum*.

G. **'Nicola'** Parentage *G.* ×*oxonianum* × *G. psilostemon*. 24 × 24 in. (60 × 60 cm). Raised by Alan Bremner, Orkney Islands, United Kingdom, and listed in the Catforth Garden catalog in 1994. The leaves are light green with five broad, overlapping lobes that have toothed margins; they appear similar to those of *G. psilostemon*. Flowers have widely separated magenta petals with a large black center. Strong black veins radiate out from the center.

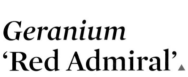

Geranium '**Red Admiral**'▲

Grows in a tallish mound, and may need some staking. The leaves are medium green with five broad lobes, and medium-large but somewhat smaller than those of G. 'Nicola'. It has deep red-magenta flowers with dark centers, a small pale central ring, and dark veins.

ZONES 5–9

PLANT SIZE 24 × 30 in. (60 × 75 cm)

SOIL Loam, neutral to slightly acidic

LIGHT Full sun in mild summer gardens, morning sun in hot summer gardens

PROPAGATION Crown division

ORIGIN Possibly *G. psilostemon* × *G. sylvaticum* 'Baker's Pink'. From Catforth Gardens, United Kingdom, in 1999. Cyril Foster in Rothbury, United Kingdom, raised the plant.

GARDEN AND DESIGN USES Perennial borders, containers

NOTES The foliage turns red in the fall. It looks attractive growing through other perennials, such as asters.

Geranium renardii ◄

Forms neat mounds of gray-green pebbled leaves that are shallowly divided into five lobes. Flowers can either be white, blue, pale reddish purple, lavender-pink, or lavender-blue with purple veins, and they grow 1½ inches (3.8 cm) wide. The petals are wedge shaped and notched.

ZONES 5–10
PLANT SIZE 12–15 × 15 in. (30–38 × 38 cm)
SOIL Well-drained loam, sandy soil, or well-drained amended clay, slightly acidic to neutral
LIGHT Full sun in mild summer gardens, morning sun and afternoon shade in hot summer gardens
PROPAGATION Seed for species, crown division for cultivars
ORIGIN Found in the Caucasus among rock cliffs. Walter Ingwersen introduced it in 1935.
GARDEN AND DESIGN USES Front of perennial borders, containers, and low-growing accents anywhere in the garden that receives morning sun
CULTIVARS
G. renardii **'Heidi Morris'** 10 × 12 in. (25 × 30 cm). From Croftway Nursery, United Kingdom, in 2001. It has lavender flowers with branching dark purple veins.
G. renardii **'Tcschelda'** 12 × 15 in. (30 × 38 cm). From Gartnerei Simon, Germany, in 1993. Hans Simon collected this around 1980. The plant has pink-blue flowers with heavy purple veins. It is frequently mixed up in the nursery trade: it is sold with lavender-blue flowers and confused with *G.* 'Terre Franche' and *G.* 'Philippe Vapelle'.
G. renardii **'Walter Ingwersen'** 12–15 × 15 in. (30–38 × 38 cm). This is the name given to the geranium sold as *G. renardii* in the United States. It has whitish flowers with purple veins. The petals are widely separated and notched. It was collected by Walter Ingwersen in the Caucasus in 1935.
G. renardii **'Whiteknights'** ◄ 10 × 12 in. (25 × 30 cm). Raised by Reading University in 1975 from wild collected seed obtained through a seed exchange, and named after its botanic garden. It has medium blue flowers.
G. renardii **'Zetterlund'** 10 × 12 in. (25 × 30 cm). Henrik Zetterlund, Gothenburg Botanic Garden, collected this on Mount Elbrus, Caucasus. The flowers are a pale red-purple with violet veins.
HYBRIDS
G. **'Chantilly'**

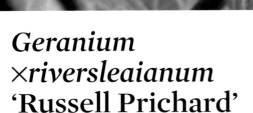

Geranium ×riversleaianum 'Russell Prichard'

A mounding and trailing perennial with gray-green five- to seven-lobed leaves. Its blue-magenta flowers, which are about 1 inch (2.5 cm) wide, grow on long trailing flowering stems.

ZONES 8–10

PLANT SIZE 18×36 in. (45×90 cm)

SOIL Moderately moist loam, sandy soil or amended clay with good drainage, slightly acidic to neutral

LIGHT Full sun in mild summer gardens, morning sun and afternoon shade in hot summer gardens.

PROPAGATION Crown division

ORIGIN *G. endressii* × *G. traversii*. Russell Prichard at Riverslea Nursery, United Kingdom, raised it before 1915.

GARDEN AND DESIGN USES Perennial borders, walls, containers

NOTES Lift and divide plants about every three years to maintain flowering and vigor. This is a very useful and long-flowering perennial.

Geranium 'Rozanne'

A large mounding plant with leaves that are slightly marbled and have five slightly overlapping lobes with prominently toothed margins. Its beautiful lilac-blue flowers have purple-lilac veins and a pale center.

ZONES 5–10
PLANT SIZE 18–36 × 24–48 in. (45–90 × 90–122 cm)
SOIL Well-drained and fertile, acidic to neutral to alkaline
LIGHT Full sun in mild summer gardens, to morning sun and afternoon shade in hot summer gardens
PROPAGATION Restricted to licensed propagators
ORIGIN Probably *G. wallichianum* 'Buxton's Variety' × an unnamed form of *G. himalayense*. Donald and Rozanne Waterer, United Kingdom, bred the plant, and Blooms of Bressingham, United Kingdom, patented it. A Dutch hybrid, *G.* 'Jolly Bee', with similar parentage, was replaced by *G.* 'Rozanne', and is no longer available.

GARDEN AND DESIGN USES It has multiple uses in the garden, including perennial beds, shrub borders, as a ground cover, and in large containers and hanging baskets. It is unquestionably one of the most successful geraniums ever produced. Many hundreds of thousands are sold each year.

NOTES Flowering is profuse and lasts from late spring through to the first frosts. In hot weather the flowers are sometimes tinged lavender-pink. Their color changes to lilac-blue in cooler temperatures in the evening and early morning. This plant takes two to three years to build up to a good size in the garden, so be patient. The first year after planting it will make some roots and few flowers, the next year will be better, and the third year you can invite the neighbors to admire it.

CULTIVARS
G. 'Azure Rush'
G. 'Lilac Ice'

Geranium 'Sabani Blue'

A mound of deeply cut dark green leaves that have five to seven over-lapping lobes. Deep violet-blue flowers with a small, pale center and dark veins.

ZONES 5–9
PLANT SIZE 18 × 24 in. (45 × 60 cm)
SOIL Moderately moist loam, sand or amended clay, slightly acidic to neutral
LIGHT Full sun in mild summer gardens, morning sun and afternoon shade in hot summer gardens
PROPAGATION Restricted to licensed propagators
ORIGIN *G. libani* × *G. ibericum* subsp. *jubatum*. Alan Bremner, Orkney Islands, United Kingdom, introduced this in 2006.
GARDEN AND DESIGN USES Perennial border in an area where early spring flowers are required
NOTES Flowers early in the spring. Plants will sometimes rebloom in the fall if planted in a cool summer garden.

Geranium sanguineum ▶

A mounding herbaceous perennial with dark green fingered leaves and fleshy underground rhizomatous roots. It forms a rosette whose leaves are rounded and partially dissected. These differ from the leaves on the flowering stems, which are divided almost to the base into narrow lobes. The color of the flowers on the species varies from white to palest pink to vibrant rose-magenta. The flowers are grow 1¼ inches (3.1 cm) wide and are saucer shaped and borne singly.

ZONES 4–10, heat and humidity tolerant
PLANT SIZE 6–34 × 10–24 in. (15–85 × 25–60 cm)
SOIL Well-drained sandy, loam, or clay soils, slightly acidic to neutral to alkaline
LIGHT Full sun to light shade
PROPAGATION Propagation from the fleshy roots is effortless, true to the named selection and recommended (although it also seeds freely). Save the seedlings you like, but remember there are many listed variations on pink and magenta with cultivar names.
ORIGIN The species is found over a wide area across Europe. It grows on dry scrubby slopes, in deciduous woodlands, and on arid grasslands from the west up to the Caucasus and in northern Turkey.
GARDEN AND DESIGN USES This plant shows excellent fall color in cold climates, and its common name, bloody cranesbill, may derive from the red color of the leaves in autumn. It flowers in flushes with the main display in the spring. When planting in the garden, count on at least three years of growth before an optimum display.
NOTES This plant should be in everyone's garden. Pruning the flowering stems reduces blooming, so do not cut back until the end of the growing season. At low temperatures it is deciduous. It has been in cultivation in the United States since at least the 1880s. It is not impervious to deer or rabbits, although it is not a particular attractant.
VARIETIES
G. sanguineum* var. *striatum ▶ 8 × 15 in. (20 × 38 cm). Originally discovered on Walney Island, Cumbria, United Kingdom, in 1670, according to Penny Clifton. It may still be found there today, growing among sand dunes. It is an excellent, neat, and compact perennial border plant with pale pink flowers and deep pink veins.

CULTIVARS The species is variable in nature and in gardens, and there are well more than 50 named selections based on plant size and small differences in flower color. Not all the selections of *G. sanguineum* are worthy of naming, and some named plants are virtually indistinguishable. There are many seed grown forms in the nursery trade. The best selections are listed.

G. sanguineum **'Album'** ▼ 34 × 24 in. (85 × 60 cm). Walter Ingwersen originally described this as *G. sanguineum* var. *album* in 1946. It is probably of garden origin, according to *Register of Geranium Cultivar Names*. Growth is somewhat open. The flowers are white with no hint of another color.

G. sanguineum **'Ankum's Pride'** ▲ 8 × 15 in. (20 × 38 cm). Coen Jansen of Coen Vaste Planten, Netherlands, raised this in 1988 as a seedling from *G. sanguineum* 'Jubilee Pink' and named it after his village. Compact growth and vivid pink flowers.

G. sanguineum **'Apfelblüte'** ◄ 12 × 18 in. (30 × 45 cm). Ernst Pagels made this selection of *G. sanguineum* 'Splendens' in the early 1980s. Beautiful palest pink flowers with a slightly darker pink wash on the outer edge of the petals.

G. sanguineum 'Bloody Graham' 18 × 20 in. (45 × 50 cm). From Monksilver Nursery, United Kingdom, in 1993. It was a garden seedling from Graham Stuart Thomas. Large medium magenta-pink flowers.

G. sanguineum 'Canon Miles' ▼ 4 × 8 in. (10 × 20 cm). From John Anton Smith, United Kingdom, and first published in 1997. Very compact growth with medium pink flowers that have a lighter ring around the outer edge of the petals and light purple veins.

G. sanguineum 'Cedric Morris' ▶ 30 × 24 in. (75 × 60 cm). Sir Cedric Morris collected this from the Gower Coast, Wales, before 1994. A large vigorous plant with flowers that are light magenta-pink with purple veins.

G. sanguineum 'Cricklewood' 18–24 × 60 in. (45–60 × 150 cm). Found at the Cricklewood Nursery, United States, and raised by Dennis Thompson. The description was published in 1991. It is a vigorous plant with *G. sanguineum* type leaves and magenta-pink flowers. It tolerates some drought.

G. sanguineum 'Droplet' ▶ (syn. *G. sanguineum* 'Minutum') 2 × 8 in. (5 × 20 cm). The name was given by *Register of Geranium Cultivar Names* in 2004 for a plant incorrectly named *G. sanguineum* 'Minutum'. The most compact *G. sanguineum*, with small light pink flowers with rose veins.

G. sanguineum **'Elke'** ▲ 12 × 18 in. (30 × 45 cm). Geert Lambrecht purchased this garden seedling from a nursery in Belgium, and first published it in 2005. Strong pink flowers with a small white eye and a pale outer edge to the petals.

G. sanguineum **'Elsbeth'** 30 × 24 in. (75 × 60 cm). A wild collection by Hans Simon, Switzerland, distributed in 1982. Medium green hairy, finely dissected leaves, and medium magenta-pink flowers.

G. sanguineum **'Glenluce'** ▶ 18 × 20 in. (45 × 50 cm). A. T. Johnson collected this near Glenluce, Scotland, before 1937. Wild rose-pink flowers with a slight bluish cast, and light purple veins.

G. sanguineum 'John Elsley' ▶ 12 × 18 in. (30 × 45 cm). From Blooms of Bressingham, United Kingdom, in 1993. Floriferous selection with light magenta-pink flowers.

G. sanguineum 'Kristin Jakob' ▼ 15 × 18 in. (38 × 45 cm). Kristin Jakob selected this from a group of plants at Sloat Nursery in San Rafael, California, in 1991, and Geraniaceae Nursery, California, named it after her. A mounding plant with fine purple-magenta flowers, prominent purple veins and a small white center.

***G. sanguineum* 'Max Frei'** ▲ 6 × 10 in. (15 × 25 cm). From the Hans Frei Nursery, Germany, in 1976. This was a seedling found in Max Frei's alpine garden in Switzerland. A neat, compact plant with rose-magenta flowers.

***G. sanguineum* 'Nyewood'** 10–14 × 15 in. (25–36 × 38 cm). From Monksilver Nursery, United Kingdom, 1994. This has strong blue-pink flowers.

***G. sanguineum* 'Shepherd's Warning'** ◄ 8 × 15 in. (20 × 38 cm). Raised by Jack Drake, Scotland, in 1975. Small, vibrant, cerise-pink flowers on a low-growing vigorous plant.

HYBRIDS

***G.* 'Blushing Turtle'** (syn. 'Breathless')

***G.* 'Dilys'**

***G.* 'Diva'**

***G.* 'Khan'**

***G.* 'Tiny Monster'**

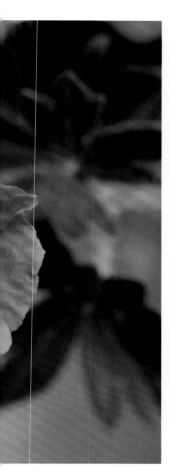

Geranium 'Sellindge Blue'

A mounding geranium with medium green leaves that have strong veins and seven broad lobes with deeply cut divisions and sharp teeth. It has large blue flowers with slightly darker veins and spoon-shaped petals.

ZONES 5–9

PLANT SIZE 30 × 24 in. (76 × 60 cm)

SOIL Moderately moist loam, mildly acidic to neutral

LIGHT Full sun in mild summer gardens, morning sun and afternoon shade in hot summer gardens

PROPAGATION Crown division

ORIGIN Possibly *G. pratense* × *G. saxatile*. Found in the garden of Martin Rix at Sellindge, Kent, United Kingdom.

GARDEN AND DESIGN USES Perennial borders, containers

Geranium 'Sirak'. ▲

A large mound with broad bright green leaves that have seven lobes. The flowers are 2 inches (5 cm) in diameter and are dusky deep pink with very prominent purple eyelash veins. The petals are notched and the center of the flower is a whitish color.

ZONES 5–9
PLANT SIZE 15–18 × 24 in. (38–45 × 60 cm)
SOIL Moderately moist loam, slightly acidic to neutral
LIGHT Full sun in mild summer gardens, morning sun and afternoon shade in hot summer gardens
PROPAGATION Crown division
ORIGIN Possibly *G. gracile* × *G. ibericum*. Raised by Hans Simon, Marktheidenfeld, Germany, around 1992. Alan Bremner raised a very similar plant and gave it the cultivar name 'Karis'.
GARDEN AND DESIGN USES Perennial borders, containers

Geranium soboliferum ◄

Mounds of ferny, finely dissected leaves that have five to seven narrow lobes. Flowers are 1½ to 1¾ inches (3.8–4.4 cm) in diameter and saucer shaped with dark red-pink petals and hairs visible on the upper petal surface. It flowers late in the summer.

ZONES 5–9
PLANT SIZE 18–24 × 24 in. (45–60 × 60 cm)
SOIL Moderate loam, moist and well-drained, slightly acidic to neutral
LIGHT Full sun in mild summer gardens, morning sun and afternoon shade in hot summer gardens
PROPAGATION Crown division, seed (propagation of named varieties is restricted to licensed propagators)
ORIGIN Russian Federation, Manchuria, Korea, and the mountains of central and southern Japan.
GARDEN AND DESIGN USES Perennial borders
NOTES This is a useful plant for a late summer garden. The leaves take on a pleasing cinnamon color in the fall. Make sure to plant it in damp soil.
CULTIVARS
G. soboliferum **'Butterfly Kisses'** 18 × 24–36 in. (45 × 60–90 cm). From Intrinsic Perennial Gardens, Illinois, in 2010. This large, sprawling plant has deep pink flowers with an intricate network of purple veins and some deeper shading of pink underneath them.
G. soboliferum **'Starman'** 15 × 24 in. (38 × 60 cm). Rolf Offenthal, Grethem, Germany, developed this in 1999. It has a compact habit and upright flowering stems. Its dark red-pink flowers have purple veins and long deep red-purple blotches on each petal. Flowers are 1¾ inches (4.4 cm) in diameter. It flowers from June to September.

Geranium 'Spinners' ▲

A large billowing mound. The medium green leaves resemble *G. pratense* and are finely dissected. New foliage emerges in the spring with a faint yellow cast, which disappears as it matures. The flowers are deep purple with red veins, bowl shaped, and upturned.

ZONES 5–9
PLANT SIZE 30 × 36 in. (75 × 90 cm)
SOIL Moderately damp loam, amended clay, acidic to neutral to alkaline
LIGHT Full sun in mild summer gardens, morning sun and afternoon shade in hot summer gardens
PROPAGATION Crown division (*G.* 'Spinners' is largely sterile)
ORIGIN Exact parentage is unknown. Peter Chappell of Spinners Nursery, United Kingdom, raised the plant from seed collected by Marvin Black of Seattle.
GARDEN AND DESIGN USES Perennial borders, front of shrub borders, massed plantings, large mixed plant containers
NOTES Tolerates heat and humidity. It needs some support when it is young, as it has a tendency to flop.

Geranium 'Sue Crûg'

Leaves are five lobed, broad, and toothed. Flowers are a red-purple with a dark center. The petals are separated and have a pale central stripe and dark veins.

ZONES 6–9, possibly lower
PLANT SIZE 18 × 24 in. (45 × 60 cm). It is a spreading loose mound. The leaves are medium green, broadly and deeply lobed. Cut back after flowering to produce new leaves and flowers.
SOIL Moderate well-drained loam, slightly acidic to neutral
LIGHT Full sun in mild summer gardens, morning sun and afternoon shade in hot summer gardens
PROPAGATION Crown division
ORIGIN Possibly *G.* ×*oxonianum* × *G.* 'Salome'. Bleddyn Wynn-Jones of Crûg Farm Plants, Wales, raised the plant and named it for his wife. Published in the Crûg Farm Plants Catalog in 1993.
GARDEN AND DESIGN USES Perennial borders, containers
NOTES Cut back after flowering to produce new leaves and flowers.

Geranium 'Summer Cloud'

Mounding plant with medium green leaves that have seven deeply cut lobes; the center lobes are shorter than those on the sides. The flowers have single white, spoon-shaped petals with lavender veins. The flowers resemble those of *G. clarkei* 'Kashmir White', but are smaller.

ZONES 5–9
PLANT SIZE 24 × 24 in. (60 × 60 cm)
SOIL Moderate loam, neutral to slightly alkaline
LIGHT Full sun in mild summer gardens, morning sun and afternoon shade in hot summer gardens
PROPAGATION Crown division
ORIGIN Possibly *G. collinum* × *G. clarkei* 'Kashmir White'. It was a chance seedling from the Cambridge University Botanic Garden, first described in the Axletree Nursery, United Kingdom, catalog in 1998.
GARDEN AND DESIGN USES Perennial borders, large mixed plant containers
NOTES Reportedly flowers later than *G. clarkei*.

Geranium 'Terre Franche'

Compact mounds of sage green leaves that are quilted and soft with five broad and shallowly toothed lobes. It has lavender-blue flowers with purple veins and notched, separated petals.

ZONES 5–9
PLANT SIZE 10 × 15 in. (25 × 38 cm)
SOIL Moderate loam, mildly acidic to neutral
LIGHT Full sun in mild summer gardens, morning sun and afternoon shade in hot summer gardens
PROPAGATION Crown division
ORIGIN Possibly G. 'Philippe Vapelle' × G. platypetalum. Ivan Louette, Belgium, raised this and first published it in 1997.
GARDEN AND DESIGN USES Perennial borders, containers, massed plantings, border edges, rock gardens
NOTES More compact than G. 'Philippe Vapelle', which it closely resembles. Plants of this name may be confused in the trade with 'Philippe Vapelle'.

Geranium transbaicalicum

Looks like a form of G. pratense, but it is lower growing and the leaf divisions are finer with five to seven narrow, deeply cut, toothed lobes. It often produces dark red stems. Flowers are a light blue with dark veins. Lower-growing selections are elegant and desirable, but the plant becomes progressively more like G. pratense through its range.

ZONES 5–9
PLANT SIZE 10 × 18 in. (25 × 45 cm)
SOIL Medium loam, slightly acidic to neutral
LIGHT Full sun in mild summer gardens, morning sun and afternoon shade in hot summer gardens
PROPAGATION Crown division, seed. Experiment with seed collections from different areas to find the most compact selection.
ORIGIN China, Mongolia, Siberia, east and west of Lake Baikal, the Russian Federation
GARDEN AND DESIGN USES Front of a perennial border, rock garden, or alpine trough

TUBEROUS-ROOTED SPECIES

Tuberous rooted geraniums seem like an anomaly in the genus Geranium, and they are challenging to collect and fascinating to grow. The species from China require regular culture and summer water, while those from mountainous areas of Turkey, Iran, and central Asia need a period of summer dormancy. The inviolate rule for the latter group is *no summer water at all*. To ensure these plants are not watered, either place their containers in a cool, dry situation for the summer after they become dormant, or lift them from the ground and store them in an inert material, such as sand, until planting time in fall. Identification of the different species from the shape of the tubers is one of the pleasures of these plants. *Geranium tuberosum* tubers looks like lumpy little potatoes, *G. transversale* is scorpion-like, *G. malviflorum* resembles a spaceship, and *G. libani* has a more conventional rhizomatous root. The Chinese tuberous geraniums have small, round, pea-like tubers.

Plant widths depend on the number of tubers in the area. The tubers produce few leaves and solitary flowering stems. In some species, however, the tubers will multiply rapidly and cover quite large areas of ground.

Geranium libani ▶

Mounds of glossy light green leaves with five to seven broad and deeply toothed lobes. Plants have 18-inch (45 cm) flowering stems and spreading underground rhizomes. The flowers are 1½ inches (3.8 cm) and medium lavender-blue with notched petals and feathered veins. They appear on stems held well above the leaves. They flower in spring and are semi-dormant in summer.

ZONES 8–10
PLANT SIZE 10 in. (25 cm) high
SOIL Well-drained loam to rocky; it prefers neutral to alkaline but will also tolerate lightly acidic soil. Requires semi-dry soil in the summer.
LIGHT Full sun
PROPAGATION Division by root, seed
ORIGIN Native to Lebanon, central southern Turkey and western Syria, in fir forests, oak scrub, and grassy areas near limestone cliffs and gorges.
GARDEN AND DESIGN USES Rock gardens, containers, and well-drained perennial gardens or borders that receive no water in the summer.
NOTES Will tolerate a small amount of summer water if the drainage is excellent. In mild winter gardens, leaves appear in late fall and it flowers early the following year.

Geranium malviflorum ▲

Spreads from underground tubers, but unlike *G. tuberosum*, it does not become too invasive. It grows large horizontal, spindle-shaped tubers and handsome leaves that are divided into seven lobes, each lobe further divided into narrow, pointed, and toothed divisions. The violet-blue flowers have dark veins and grow up to 1½ inches (3.8 cm) across. Leaves will appear in the fall and the plant will grow through the winter and flower in the spring; it is summer dormant.

ZONES 7–10, possibly lower
PLANT SIZE 12 in. (30 cm) high
SOIL Well-drained loam, neutral to slightly alkaline
LIGHT Full sun
PROPAGATION Tubers, seed
ORIGIN Southern Spain, Morocco, Algeria
GARDEN AND DESIGN USES Rock gardens, containers. Allow to go dormant in the summer.
NOTES No summer water.
CULTIVARS
G. malviflorum **'Sweetheart'** 9–12 in. (23–30 cm). Edelweiss Perennials, Oregon, selected this form, which has heart-shaped petals and pink flowers.

Geranium tuberosum ▸

Grows from rapidly spreading tubers with several finely divided leaves that are deeply dissected, five- to seven-lobed, and toothed. There are tall-flowering stems up to 12 inches (30 cm) in height with 1-inch (2.5 cm) rosy lilac flowers fading to cool lilac in the center with darker veins. The petals are notched and separated. The tuber is usually horizontal under the ground and looks like a small lumpy potato.

ZONES 8–10
PLANT SIZE 12 in. (30 cm) high
SOIL Wide range of soils from amended clay to loam to sandy. Neutral, and possibly slightly acidic or slightly alkaline. Moderate water during growth, no water during summer dormancy.
LIGHT Full sun
PROPAGATION Tubers, seed
ORIGIN From the Mediterranean to western Iran. It is often a plant of disturbed places, roadsides, and cultivated ground such as fields.
GARDEN AND DESIGN USES Rock gardens, containers
NOTES Easy to obtain from bulb catalogs. Because of its very large range, leaf shapes tend to vary depending on the location of the collection. Plants become dormant in summer, growing and flowering during late winter and early spring. You can store tubers during summer to avoid water and then replant them in the winter or early spring, depending on the severity of winter.

SUBSPECIES

G. tuberosum subsp. linearifolium Grows up to 12 in. (30 cm) tall. Unlike the typical species, the divisions of the basal leaf are totally separated. The stems have alternate silver-gray leaves, and the leaf divisions are narrower and more serrated. The flowers are pink-purple and appear in late spring. It needs sun, and may be grown in a rock garden or area of scree. It is found in Turkey, the Caucasus, Iran, and Syria.

G. tuberosum subsp. tuberosum Grows up to 12 in. (30 cm) tall. Distinguished from the species by its leafless stems. It is found in the Mediterranean west of Iran, on rocky slopes in scrub and woods, up to 6500 feet (1980 m) elevation.

CULTIVARS

G. tuberosum 'Richard Hobbs' 12 in. (30 cm) tall. It has gray-green leaves and lavender flowers with purple veins.

Geranium orientaltibeticum ▲

Small underground tubers are linked by thin stoloniferous roots. The leaves come from the tubers and the stems are usually solitary. The yellow-green foliage is strongly marbled and deeply divided into five lobes. The flowers are medium pink with a white center and grow 1 inch (2.5 cm) wide.

ZONES 8–10
PLANT SIZE 10 in. (25 cm) high
SOIL Well-drained loam, or scree, slightly acidic to neutral
LIGHT Full sun in mild summer gardens, morning sun/afternoon shade in hot summer gardens
PROPAGATION Tubers, seed
ORIGIN It comes from Tatsien-lou, Sichuan, southwest China; grows in scrub
GARDEN AND DESIGN USES Rock gardens, containers, front of a perennial border
NOTES The marbled leaves are very attractive in the garden, but it spreads easily, so take care not to dig in the area where it is located and further scatter the tubers.

ANNUALS

Annual and biennial geraniums have a special niche in the garden, as they fill bare spaces where other plants may struggle to survive. Usually annuals are not fussy about soil, although you can achieve larger and more lush plants in well-drained humusy soil. After flowering, leave seed heads on for a period, then cut and lay over the ground so the seeds will establish for the following year. In mild winter areas, you can sow seed in fall; in colder climates, do so in early spring. Carefully transport relatively small plants from seed trays to locations where they are to grow.

Geranium brutium

SYNONYM *G. molle*

Grows upright with flowers on long pedicels, and reseeds mildly. Leaves are small, broadly lobed, and rounded. Bright pink flowers have purple veins and deeply notched petals. They are ½ inch (1.25 cm) in diameter.

ZONES Annual
PLANT SIZE 10 × 12 in. (25 × 30 cm)
SOIL Dryish soil, loam, amended clay, light sandy soil, slightly acidic to neutral
LIGHT Morning sun and afternoon shade
PROPAGATION Seed. Sow in place, or plant out after last frost.
ORIGIN From southern Italy, Greece, Serbia, and Turkey. As part of his botanical revision of Geraniaceae, Carlos Aedo has collapsed the name *G. brutium* into *G. molle*, but *G. brutium* has larger and far showier flowers. Name confusion can pose a problem for gardeners: If you order *G. molle* from a seed source, you will end up with a roadside weed. Try to obtain a named packet of seed of *G. brutium*, at least for the time being.
GARDEN AND DESIGN USES Wild garden, among bulbs, in a shrub border

Geranium yeoi

SYNONYM G. rubescens

An annual or short-lived perennial with a large rosette of dark green highly lobed and dissected leaves. The foliage takes on red tones during fall and early winter. It looks something like an overgrown G. robertianum. It has many 1-inch (2.5 cm) bright pink flowers with a darker pink streak in the center of each petal. It blooms on thick reddish flowering stems for a long time.

ZONES 8–10
PLANT SIZE 24 × 36 in. (60 × 90 cm)
SOIL It will grow anywhere, loam, clay or sandy soil, but usually does best in well-drained loam, mildly acidic to neutral
LIGHT Morning sun to light shade
PROPAGATION Seed
ORIGIN From Madeira
GARDEN AND DESIGN USES For a wild garden or a garden in light shade. It is attractive, but can be difficult to eradicate because of its many seedlings.
NOTES Frost can kill this plant, but it usually seeds prolifically.

Geranium ocellatum

Low sprawling annual. The leaves have five to seven lobes that are profusely toothed. Its small, brilliant magenta flowers feature a black eye. The Asian forms are more prostrate than the African ones, which tend to be erect.

ZONES Annual
PLANT SIZE 6–12 × 15–30 in. (15–30 × 38–75 cm)
SOIL Grows in all soil types
LIGHT Sun to shade
PROPAGATION Seed
ORIGIN Found from western Africa to eastern Africa, and from southwest China to the Himalayas. It grows in shady as well as sunny locations.
GARDEN AND DESIGN USES For any area of the garden that is sunny to partly shady. It seeds moderately and, once established, returns year after year.

NORTH AMERICAN SPECIES

They grow in our backyard, if the wilderness could be considered our backyard, and yet with a few exceptions, they are rarely found in the garden. The North American geraniums are most frequently plants of hilly or mountainous areas. Their flowers are not overwhelming in size or color but they are easy to grow and form attractive mounds in the garden. There are also a number of weedy native and European species found all over North America that we can safely ignore.

Geranium maculatum is found in many areas of the east coast and is probably the most widespread of our native geraniums in gardens. There are a number of selected color forms and several with brown or reddish brown leaves. *Geranium caespitosum*, *G. californicum*, *G. erianthum*, *G. oreganum*, *G. richardsonii*, and *G. viscosissimum* are found in the western states.

One can only sigh about the Hawaiian geraniums. All but one are critically endangered and all require such specific growing conditions that they have proved impossible to cultivate in botanical or home gardens. If you visit Hawaii you can view some of them in their natural surroundings. They are a fascinating group of woody shrubs, and some are found in inhospitable wetlands with very high rainfall. They include *G. arboretum*, *G. cuneatum*, *G. hanaense*, *G. hillebrandii*, *G. kauaiense*, and *G. multiflorum*, but they are not in cultivation.

Geranium californicum

A large, billowy plant with medium gray-green seven-lobed leaves with very few teeth. It has medium to pale pink flowers that become lighter in the center and have prominent red-purple veins, 1–1½ inches (2.5–3.8 cm) diameter. It blooms from spring to late summer.

ZONES 5–9
PLANT SIZE 15 × 24 in. (38 × 60 cm)
SOIL Slightly damp to dryish loam, acidic to neutral
LIGHT Morning sun and afternoon shade
PROPAGATION Seed
ORIGIN Endemic to California, coastal ranges, southern Sierra Nevada, pine forests, and wetlands at elevations around 8000 feet (2440 m).
GARDEN AND DESIGN USES Over walls, in containers, in wild gardens where there is morning sun and afternoon shade. Flowers from April to August.
NOTES Needs good drainage and only light summer watering. You can find numerous seedlings in areas where it is happy. Some plants in the field have powdery mildew, but this has not been observed in nursery stock.

Geranium erianthum ◄

Tall, vase-shaped plants with seven to nine broadly lobed large leaves whose lobes are overlapping. Flowers on tall 18- to 24-inch (45–60 cm) stems in a variety of colors, some of which have cultivar names. Flowers can vary from white to pale to dark blue, and veins can be clear, blue, pink, or purple.

ZONES 3–9
PLANT SIZE 12–24 × 18 in. (30–60 × 45 cm)
SOIL Well-drained loam to sandy and heavy amended clay, slightly acidic to neutral
LIGHT Full sun in mild summer gardens, morning sun and afternoon shade in hot summer gardens
PROPAGATION Crown division, seed if flower color is not important
ORIGIN From eastern Siberia, Kuril Isles, Sakhalin Island, Japan, Alaska, Aleutian Isles, and British Columbia, Canada. Grows in damp lowland meadows, sub-alpine meadows, scrub, and grassy slopes near the sea.
GARDEN AND DESIGN USES Perennial borders, as a cover for annual bulbs
NOTES Good fall color on the leaves in cold climates. This geranium spans continents and appears in the Far East and in North America. It is a common wildflower in Alaska and appears to adapt well to gardens in the lower 48 states. The cultivars listed are selections from the Far East, but there is considerable variation in flower color and venation that occurs in plants grown from seed gathered in Alaska, and some seedlings have looked very similar to *G. erianthum* 'Calm Sea'. There is also an unnamed form from Alaska that has white flowers with strong pink veins.

FORMS

G. erianthum f. *leucanthum* 12 × 18 in. (30 × 45 cm). From northern Japan. It forms dense tussocks and has white flowers with separated petals.

CULTIVARS

G. erianthum **'Calm Sea'** ▲ 18 × 18 in. (45 × 45 cm). From a botanical garden in Vladivostok, Russia, via Cambridge Botanical Garden, but a similar form has arisen from seed that Marty Schwartz collected in the wild in Alaska. Flowers are pale blue-white with dark blue veins and a faint bluish zone near the center of the flower.

G. erianthum f. *leucanthum* **'Undine'** 12 × 18 in. (30 × 45 cm). A compact white-flowered form.

G. erianthum **'Neptune'** 15 × 18 in. (38 × 45 cm). From the University of Uppsala, Sweden, via a botanical garden in Japan. David Hibberd from Axletree Nursery, United Kingdom, named it. The plant has dark blue-purple flowers with translucent veins.

Geranium maculatum ▲

A mounding plant with medium green, shiny leaves that are divided almost to the base into five to seven broad lobes. The lobes are diamond shaped and toothed. Sometimes the leaves have light green blotches, but this has not been seen in cultivated forms. Flowers are held well above the leaves, and they are pale blue-pink, white, and purple; saucer shaped; and upward facing, usually with cream centers and 1¼ inches (3.1 cm) in diameter.

ZONES 4–9

PLANT SIZE 18–24 × 18 in. (45–60 × 45 cm)

SOIL Average soil with light to medium moisture and good drainage, slightly acidic to neutral

LIGHT Morning sun and afternoon shade

PROPAGATION Seed for species, crown division for cultivars; seeds readily

ORIGIN Found in the eastern United States from Maine to Georgia, west to Manitoba, South Dakota, Kansas, down to Arkansas. Can be located in dry or moist woods, woodland edges, and meadows in partial sun.

GARDEN AND DESIGN USES Use in a perennial border that gets afternoon shade, a shade garden that gets filtered light with some morning sun, or in a shrub border in bright shade.

NOTES Useful for difficult dry shade conditions under deciduous trees, but it can also tolerate well-drained but damp meadows. It has one flowering in the early spring to early summer, then remains in leaf and inconspicuous for the rest of the growing season.

FORMS

G. maculatum **f. *albiflorum*** 15 × 20 in. (38 × 50 cm). It has 1¼-inch (3.1 cm) white flowers.

CULTIVARS

***G. maculatum* 'Album'** 15 × 20 in. (38 × 50 cm). The Royal Horticultural Society dictionary originally published this as var. *album* in 1956. It has pure white flowers that are 1¼ inches (3.1 cm) in diameter.

***G. maculatum* 'Beth Chatto'** 18 × 18 in. (45 × 45 cm). Raised at Beth Chatto's Unusual Plants in Essex, United Kingdom. The Registrar of Geranium Cultivar Names gave the name in place of 'Chatto's Form'. It has large light pink flowers, 1½ inches (3.8 cm) in diameter.

***G. maculatum* 'Elizabeth Ann'** ◄ 18 × 18 in. (45 × 45 cm). Discovered by Carol (Kim) Tyssowski in Baltimore in 1994, and named for her niece. It has dark chocolate-colored leaves that turn red-brown in the fall. The flowers are medium blue-pink and 1½ inches (3.8 cm) in diameter. Restricted to licensed propagators.

***G. maculatum* 'Espresso'** 18 × 18 in. (45 × 45 cm). Dick Lighty found this at Mount Cuba, Delaware, and North Creek Nursery found it in Landeberg, Pennsylvania. It has green-brown leaves with pale pink flowers with a white eye. It needs to be grown in sun or the leaf color becomes greener. It has good fall color.

***G. maculatum* 'Hazel Gallagher'** 12 × 15 in. (30 × 38 cm). John Gallagher named it after his wife and gave it to Sunny Border in Connecticut. It is compact, with pure white flowers without a hint of pink that are 1½ inches (3.8 cm) in diameter.

***G. maculatum* 'Heronswood Gold'** 15 × 15 in. (38 × 38 cm). Heronswood Nursery, Washington, selected this plant, which has golden leaves and pale pink flowers. The foliage retains its color through the growing season.

***G. maculatum* 'Silver Buttons'** 15 × 15 in. (38 × 28 cm). The Desirable Plant Nursery, United Kingdom, first published this in 2008. Its origin is unknown. This form has dark green leaves, and white flowers with clear veins and fringed petals.

***G. maculatum* 'Spring Purple'** 15 × 20 in. (38 × 50 cm). Medium lavender flowers with purple veins and a small green-white center.

***G. maculatum* 'Sweetwater'** 18 × 18 in. (45 × 45 cm). Found at the Sweetwater Nursery in Point Richmond, California, in 1984. Its origin is unknown. It has shiny medium green leaves and light violet-pink flowers with cream centers.

***G.* 'Vickie Lynn'** 12 × 24 in. (30 × 60 cm). Selected in Switzerland by Edelweiss Perennials of Oregon. It has glossy maroon-red fall color and pale pink flowers that are slightly larger than *G. maculatum*.

Geranium oreganum ▾

Leaves are deep green with five to seven lobes. Plants have a woody base, a mounding structure, and an unbranched inflorescence. It has a single to a few clusters of purple pink to blue-purple flowers that are 1 inch (2.5 cm) in diameter and face upward. It blooms late spring to midsummer.

ZONES 5–9
PLANT SIZE 15 × 24 in. (38 × 60 cm)
SOIL Loam, damp to dryish, mildly acidic to neutral
LIGHT Full sun to partial shade
PROPAGATION Seed
ORIGIN Found in mountain forests and meadows from 2300 to 5900 feet (700–1800 m) in moist and partially dry conditions in Oregon, Washington, California, and Montana.
GARDEN AND DESIGN USES Perennial border, wild garden

Geranium richardsonii ▾

A tall plant with long flowering stems; it grows from a thickened rootstock, with a few sprawling-to-erect branched stems. It has green, hairy, deeply divided, toothed, five- to seven-lobed leaves. The stems are green and somewhat stickier than *G. viscosissimum*. The flowers have broad rounded petals, 1 inch (2.5 cm) in diameter, and are white with pink veins and have hairs on the upper surfaces of the petals. There are also flowers in pale violet pink and pale lavender.

ZONES 4–9
PLANT SIZE 24–30 × 20 in. (60–75 ×50 cm)
SOIL Damp to wet loam, acidic to neutral
LIGHT Partial shade
PROPAGATION Seed
ORIGIN Native to western North America from southeastern British Columbia, eastern Washington and Oregon to California, east to New Mexico, South Dakota, and Saskatchewan. It grows in moist, shady conditions in mountain meadows and forests.
GARDEN AND DESIGN USES It is rarely used in gardens, but makes an attractive plant in a perennial garden where you can water it well.
NOTES Flowers from late spring through fall.

Geranium sp. ▲

The medium green leaves are prominent and broadly lobed into five divisions that are further divided into three. It has nodding ¾-inch (1.9 cm) cherry red flowers with blue pollen.

ZONES 6–9
PLANT SIZE 15 × 18 in. (38 × 45 cm)
SOIL Slightly dry, well-drained, light loam, slightly acidic to neutral
LIGHT Full sun in mild summer gardens, morning sun and afternoon shade in hot summer gardens
PROPAGATION Roots, seed
ORIGIN Found in seed collected in the Sangre de Cristo Mountains, New Mexico, and labelled *G. caespitosum*. Dennis Breedlove, Academy of Sciences, San Francisco, collected it in Durango, Mexico, in 1979 and it grows at University of California Berkeley Botanic Garden under the same name.
GARDEN AND DESIGN USES Rock garden, well-drained perennial borders
NOTES There is considerable confusion about the name of this plant, which is invalidly known as *G. caespitosum*. It does not appear to be listed in Carlos Aedo's revision of the North American geraniums, and the red color of the flowers is highly unusual. The plants of this geranium and the true *G. caespitosum* look somewhat similar when out of flower, although they are unmistakably different when in bloom. It is easy to grow and makes a very charming and unusual plant for the garden.

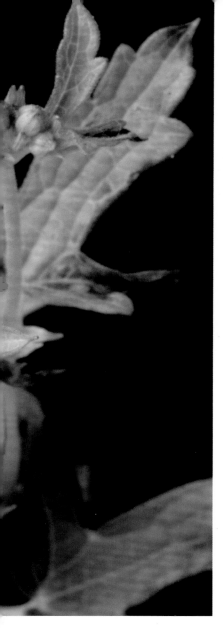

Geranium viscosissimum ▲

A tall, mounding plant with numerous flowering stems. It has gray-green large, broadly divided, five- to seven-lobed, downy-haired fragrant leaves. The plant has sticky glandular hairs that cover the stems and the leaves, and distinctive upward-facing purple-pink flowers with purple veins. The flowers are 1 to 1½ inches (2.5–3.8 cm) wide and grow in clusters. They can also be pale pink or even white.

ZONES 4–9
PLANT SIZE 20–36 × 24 in. (50–90 × 60 cm)
SOIL Loam, acidic to neutral
LIGHT Full sun to partial sun
PROPAGATION Seed. The plant has a thick rootstock that makes vegetative propagation difficult, but seeds germinate readily.
ORIGIN Western North America, from British Columbia through the Rocky Mountain States to Colorado. It grows in foothills, mountains, and subalpine regions with good drainage at medium to high elevation.
GARDEN AND DESIGN USES Perennial gardens, rock gardens
NOTES Does well in dry gardens that only receive modest supplemental irrigation during spring and summer. Foliage turns red in fall.
VARIETIES
G. viscosissimum var. *incisum* Leaves have lobes that are sharply pointed and do not have the sticky glands.

SOUTH AFRICAN SPECIES

South African geraniums are beautiful plants in their own right: large, woody subshrubs, often with gray to silver leaves and pink, lavender, and purple flowers. They are perfect for a dry, gravel, or a gray garden. All of them like some summer water. Grow them as you would their cousins, the pelargoniums: Put them outside in the garden during the growing season, then take cuttings and bring those under shelter during winter. Or test them, as the Denver Botanic Garden does, by hardening them off in the garden in autumn through reduction of water. These plants will not grow in all parts of the country, but there are some areas, particularly on the west coast and the central Rockies, where they may flourish. They are not difficult to find from a number of seed sources in South Africa.

Geranium brycei

Bushy subshrub with mounds of gray-green downy, seven-lobed leaves that are heavily veined and crowded at the branch tips. This forms a fairly compact, slightly sprawling mound. Large flowers are pale to deep violet, 1½ inches (3.8 cm), with a white patch at the base. It is not as floriferous as some of the other South African geraniums, such as *G. incanum*, but the flower and leaf colors harmonize well.

ZONES 8–10, possibly lower
PLANT SIZE 18–24 × 20 in. (45–60 × 50 cm)
SOIL Damp, rocky places with fast-draining soil, slightly acidic to neutral to alkaline
LIGHT Full sun in mild summer gardens; tolerance to hot summers in gardens is unknown
PROPAGATION Stem cuttings (tips of the woody stems, like those of a pelargonium), seed
ORIGIN From South Africa in high mountains of Lesotho, Natal Drakensberg, Cape Drakensberg, and Witteberg, at 7400 to 9800 feet (2255–2990 m); drainage lines, stream banks, and damp rocky places.
GARDEN AND DESIGN USES Containers, a silver garden in full sun with damp soil and excellent drainage
NOTES Although this plant comes from high altitude, it adapts well to garden cultivation as long as drainage is sharp.

Geranium 'Frances Grate'

A large shrubby geranium with woody lower stems and soft gray-green new wood. Leaves are finely dissected, gray-green above and silvery below. Flowers are pale lilac-mauve, 1 inch (2.5 cm) across with dark veins. They are very attractive in combination with the foliage. It makes a large weed-smothering ground cover.

ZONES 8–10
PLANT SIZE 12–18 × 60–72 in. (30–45 × 150–183 cm)
SOIL Well-drained, damp to dryish, acid or alkaline
LIGHT Full sun in all but the hottest summer gardens, where it should be given morning sun and afternoon shade
PROPAGATION Stem cuttings
ORIGIN Frances Grate discovered this plant in her garden in Monterey, California. Geraniaceae Nursery, California, named it for her in the late 1980s. Possibly *G. incanum* × *G. robustum*, both of which were growing in the garden.
GARDEN AND DESIGN USES This plant can cover large areas in the garden. Place it where it cannot overrun small perennials, such as sunny shrub borders or the back of perennial borders.
HYBRIDS There are a number of named hybrids of *G. incanum* and *G. robustum*. They seed profusely, although the offspring appear generally similar.
G. **'Rambling Robin'** 12–18 × 60–72 in. (30–45 × 150–183 cm). A seedling of *G. incanum* × *G. robustum*, raised by Robin Moss, United Kingdom, and published by Axletree Nursery, United Kingdom, in 1996. It has lavender-pink flowers with a small pale center.
G. **'Silver Cloak'** 18 × 24 in. (45 × 60 cm). A seed strain from Plant World Seeds, United Kingdom, in 2004. It is said to be a cross between *G. incanum* and *G. robustum*. The flowers range from pink to red-pink and the leaves are silver.
G. **'Silver Sugar Plum'** Appears to be an alternate name for *G.* 'Frances Grate'.

Geranium harveyi

Forms a clump that is woody below and has long trailing stems above. Small dissected and lobed leaves, cut almost to the base, are gray-green with a silvery sheen above and silvery below. Flowers are small, 1¼ inches (3.1 cm), and pale purple-blue with a small white center. The overall effect of the silvery leaves is the most distinctive feature of the plant.

ZONES 8–10
PLANT SIZE 12 × 36 in. (30 × 90 cm)
SOIL Well-drained, damp to dryish soil, acid or alkaline
LIGHT Full sun in all but the hottest summer gardens, where it should be given morning sun and afternoon shade
PROPAGATION Seed, stem cuttings
ORIGIN Found in the Transkei region of Eastern Cape province in South Africa, in mountains between 4200 and 6500 feet (1280–1980 m) and among rocks and bushes on grassy slopes.
GARDEN AND DESIGN USES The flowers are relatively insignificant in size and are not profuse. Grow the plant for its trailing mounds of silvery leaves, and place it in a dryish part of a border, over a wall, or in a container.
NOTES *Do not overwater*. It is probably not hardy below 25°F (−3.9°C), so cuttings should be rooted and held over winter to be replanted in the spring.

Geranium incanum

A dense mounding and trailing evergreen perennial with a long, thickened taproot with thin woody stems below and seasonal stems of light green above. It has very finely dissected leaves with five lobes that are medium green on top and silver-green below. Masses of mauve, red-purple, pink, or white flowers measure 1 to 1¼ inches (2.5–3.1 cm) across. In cold climates leaves will become reddish. In mild climates it flowers nine months of the year. The plant does not require heavy watering, and you can allow it to go somewhat dry between waterings.

ZONES 9–10

PLANT SIZE 12–20 × 24 in. (30–50 × 60 cm)

SOIL Light sandy loam, dryish, acidic to neutral

LIGHT Full sun to morning sun and afternoon shade; will tolerate stand hot afternoon sun in hot summer gardens

PROPAGATION Seed, stem cuttings

ORIGIN South Africa in the Western and Eastern Capes at low altitudes.

GARDEN AND DESIGN USES Containers, ground cover, perennial borders, over rock walls

NOTES Seeds very freely, so take care to place it in areas where you can easily remove seedlings. It is not suitable for rock gardens as the seeds can tuck themselves in between rocks. Prune lightly to shape, but do not cut back too far into old brown wood, which may kill the plant outright.

VARIETIES

G. incanum var. *incanum* 8–12 × 36–48 in. (20–30 × 90–122 cm). Common on flats, hills, slopes and dunes of South Africa's Western and Eastern Cape Peninsula, east to Knysna. It has small white or light pink flowers with dark veins.

G. incanum var. *multifidum* 12–15 × 36–72 in. (30–38 × 90–183 cm). Found only in South Africa's Eastern Province in coastal districts as far as Port Alfred. It has larger light red-purple to magenta pink flowers with a small white center.

CULTIVARS

G. incanum var. *incanum* 'Sinclaire' ▼ 12 × 24–30 in. (30 × 60–75 cm). Finely dissected leaves, green above, silver-green below. It has a mounding and long trailing habit and pale pink flowers with dark veins. Geraniaceae Nursery, California, named it in 2005 for Sinclaire McCredie Parer.

G. incanum var. *incanum* 'Sugar Plum' 14 × 24 in. (36 × 60 cm). Green finely dissected leaves, silver-green underneath, a mounding habit, and dark red-purple flowers with notched petals and dark veins. Monique Simone, Weidners Nursery, Encinitas, California, named it in 1994.

HYBRIDS

G. 'Frances Grate'

G. 'Rambling Robin'

G. 'Silver Cloak'

Geranium magniflorum

A neat mounding evergreen perennial with a woody rootstock and trailing stems. The basal leaves are densely ruffled, with very narrow fine segments that are green above and silver beneath; it looks like a mound of curled parsley. The flowers are in lax terminal clusters and are pink to blue-purple with a small white eye.

ZONES 5 (up to 7500 feet [2285 m]) to 10
PLANT SIZE 10 × 15 in. (25 × 38 cm)
SOIL Well-drained loam to sandy and gravelly soils, acidic to neutral
LIGHT Full sun to morning sun/afternoon shade
PROPAGATION Seed, stem cuttings
ORIGIN South Africa, North and South Drakensberg Mountains, from 6500 to 10,500 feet (1980–3200 m).
GARDEN AND DESIGN USES Rock garden, container.
NOTES Requires moderate to low water and flowers in the spring and summer.
CULTIVARS
G. magniflorum **'La Veta Lace'** ▲ 6–10 × 20 in. (15–25 × 50 cm). A selection with lavender-pink flowers by Panayoti Kelaidis from Denver Botanic Garden. Leaves are purple and scarlet during winter.

Geranium multisectum ◄

Mounding and trailing perennial. Gray-green leaves are finely divided. Flowers are in pairs at the top of long flowering stems, and are pink-mauve with dark veins. The plant becomes woody as it gets older. It blooms in the summer.

ZONES 8–10. Although the plant grows at high altitude in the mountains, its response to temperatures below 25°F (–3.9°C) is unknown.
PLANT SIZE 12–15 × 15–25 in. (30–38 × 38–61 cm)
SOIL Heavy sandy loam with summer water
LIGHT Full sun
PROPAGATION Seed, stem cuttings
ORIGIN South Africa, Eastern Cape, to Kwa-Zulu Natal, Lesotho, Eastern Free State, and Mpumalanga. Open and marshy areas of summer rainfall, 5900 to 9800 feet (1800–2990 m).
GARDEN AND DESIGN USES Perennial borders, rock gardens, containers
NOTES Light pruning will keep it looking tidy. Although it grows in damp areas, regular but not excessive watering will suffice.

Geranium pulchrum ▾

A large billowing and spreading subshrub. The stems are woody at the base, and there are many flowering stems. The leaves are large and very handsome, broadly and deeply five- to seven-lobed, hairy green above and hairy silver beneath. The flowers are held well above the leaves on long flowering stems and are pale to deep pink and 1¼ inches (3.1 cm) in diameter.

ZONES 8–10, perhaps lower
PLANT SIZE 60 × 60 in. (150 × 150 cm)
SOIL Well-drained but moist loam, sandy soil, amended clay, acidic to neutral
LIGHT Full sun in mild summer gardens; tolerance to hot summer gardens is unknown
PROPAGATION Seed, stem cuttings
ORIGIN The plant is found at quite high altitude, 5900 to 7900 feet (1800–2400 m) in South Africa from the Eastern Cape to Limpopo Province. It is found in damp or marshy ground, on stream banks or well-watered slopes.
GARDEN AND DESIGN USES Silver garden, well-watered perennial garden
NOTES This unusual geranium can be found in seed lists from South Africa, and deserves to be better known and used in the milder areas of the country. You can root stem cuttings and overwinter them inside in cold climates.

GROWING AND PROPAGATING

Long-flowering *Geranium albanum* covers wide areas in a wild garden.

M

Most geraniums are very easy to grow and propagate, and they will reward you with rapid response when you divide and plant them. The following sections guide you through the various steps in successfully growing and increasing these versatile plants.

Cultivation

Most geraniums require reasonably moist, fertile soil that drains well. A few will tolerate boggy conditions (*Geranium gracile*, *G. palustre*) and some are drought tolerant (*G. macrorrhizum*, *G. ×cantabrigiense*). Alpine geraniums (*G. argenteum* and *G.* Cinereum Group) require fast-draining soil with amendments of gravel, rock, or perlite. Most hardy geraniums flourish between Zones 5 and 9. Some do well in Zone 10 (*G.* 'Rozanne', *G.* 'Orion', *G. ×cantabrigiense*). Some work in Zones 3 and above (*G. macrorrhizum*, *G. pratense*, and some of their hybrids). *Geranium pratense* responds to a cool summer and tends to grow less vigorously when the heat rises above 86°F (30°C). Manipulating shade will help somewhat with summer heat, but humidity is the biggest obstacle to growing hardy geraniums in the higher zones. Some species are tolerant (*G.*

sanguineum), but others (*G. psilostemon* and its hybrids, *G. pratense*, or *G.* Cinereum Group) will not flourish or even survive humid conditions. *Geranium wlassovianum* and its hybrid, *G.* 'Lakwijk Star', tolerate heat and humidity, and flower summer through fall.

Hardiness

Three maps can help you decide which plants will perform best in your garden. The USDA Plant Hardiness Zone list (see page 247) is based on minimum winter temperatures, The American Horticultural Society's Plant Heat Zone Map divides the country into zones based on average high temperatures, and the Sunset regional climate zone map of the western United States suggests climates where plants will thrive year-round.

It is relatively easy to suggest minimum temperature zones for hardy geraniums, but quite difficult to fill in heat tolerance zones because of a lack of information on which plants have failed to thrive. There are some obvious indicators: Geraniums from the Himalayas and from alpine areas generally do not grow well in areas with high summer temperatures, especially those coupled with humidity. But skill and ingenuity can often overcome obstacles. For example, one gardener was determined to grow *Geranium* (Cinereum Group) 'Ballerina' in his backyard, but he lived in the Central Valley of California, where daily 100°F (38°C) daytime temperatures during the summer months are common. He used a large, fast-draining container in light shade and put in a mist spray, and the plants thrived. Not everyone is willing to go to these extremes, but it is possible to create unique environments for unusual plants.

Site

Hardy geraniums can be loosely grouped within a number of sites in the garden. These locations are not mutually exclusive, and you can move plants in and out of each category: rock gardens, ground covers, shade, borders and bedding, scramblers and crawlers, annuals. Place North American geraniums in perennial borders or as bedding plants, site South African species in areas of the garden that receive strong light and good drainage, and are well watered, and locate tuberous rooted species where there is damp and fast-draining soil, strong light, and mild winter temperatures—or at least where the tubers will not freeze and where they cannot escape into surrounding areas.

Geranium sanguineum as a sprawling ground cover in a mixed border with rosemary and Rosa 'Cornelia', in Gary Ratway and Deborah Whigham's garden.

Soil

Geraniums are remarkably adaptable to different kinds of soil. The vast majority require damp or slightly moist loam, but they can also survive in sandy soils and clay. Geraniums are generally not particular about soil pH; it can be slightly acidic to neutral to slightly alkaline. Most alpine geraniums prefer soil that is alkaline, although they will grow in neutral to slightly acidic soil as well. *Geranium* Cinereum Group will grow better in slightly alkaline soils, and you can add oyster shells, concrete chips, or light applications of lime to neutral to slightly acidic soil. *Geranium pratense* is found on calcareous soils in many locations, but has adapted to acidic soils without notable problems. However, if you have a problem with growth, try adjusting the pH. Drainage is probably more important than the soil itself, as very few geraniums will thrive in heavy, wet soil. The soil should drain quickly, so if the garden is low lying or irrigation systems provide too much water, place plants in raised areas so water drains off the roots rapidly. Containers work well for the most fussy plants.

Geraniums grown in containers will survive in most commercial potting mixes. But gardeners have their prejudices about potting soil, and mixes heavy in redwood bark are not as successful as those with a mixture of sand and loam. A traditional rock garden mix or a sandy loam with addition of pumice provides sufficient drainage for the alpine geraniums, but you can make your own mix to suit your particular needs.

Light

Geraniums need certain amounts of light to flourish. Some will grow in full sun, but the vast majority prefer morning sun and afternoon shade, particularly in hot summer gardens. Successful placement helps to produce a well-grown plant. There are infinite microclimates within gardens, so it is hard to be too specific about where to plant. If you have the patience, observe your garden through the four seasons to see where the sun shines and for how long, then decide where to site your plants. If you want to get started now, spend a little time observing the proposed location for the new plant. If the light situation looks about right for the particular geranium, go ahead and plant it.

If you need to move a plant, let its condition be your guide. If it looks full and well grown, has healthy leaves, and is producing a quantity of flowers, it is probably in the right place. If there is some leaf burn or the plant is stunted or dying off, it may be in too much sun. Conversely, if the leaf stems are elongated, flowering is sparse, and the plant looks stressed, it may need more light. In both cases, is best to cut back the plant and move it. Dig up the plant, leaving as much roots as you can, and move it, even in midseason. Make a paper shade to cover the crown for a couple of weeks, and water it well. It should revive. Avoid moving plants on very hot summer days or when nighttime temperatures are below freezing in autumn. Do not move plants in winter unless you live in a very mild climate.

Temperature

Most geraniums will survive temperatures from Zones 5 to 9, as long as they are planted in the ground, mulched, or otherwise protected. The most cold-sensitive ones—such as *Geranium traversii* from the Chatham Islands off the coast of New Zealand, *G. incancum*, and some of the other South African geraniums—will survive only in Zones 8 and above, although they have not yet been grown through a full range of temperatures. Geraniums from Madeira and the Canary Islands—namely *G. reuteri*, *G. maderense*, *G. palmatum*, and *G. yeoi*—will be killed by temperatures below 30°F (–1°C). Sometimes creating overhead protection, such as a row cover, will give up to eight degrees of frost protection, which is sufficient to enable some of the more sensitive species to survive in marginally cold climates.

A few geraniums, such as *Geranium macrorrhizum* and *G. pratense*, are cold tolerant to Zones 3 and 4. It is important in colder climates to allow the plants to acclimatize through a full growing season before the onset of winter. Container plants are not as well protected, and soil temperatures will vary much more than those in the ground. In mild climates, where the temperature is only a few degrees below freezing, you may need to shelter containers against the house, on a porch or veranda, or in a greenhouse. Geraniums that naturally go dormant in the winter can be left in the ground and mulched lightly or heavily if they are more or less growing in their correct zone. There are many different microclimates in gardens, so careful placement may gain you half a zone of protection.

Water Needs

Watering is one of the hardest things to learn about gardening. After planting, water the plant and its surrounding soil. Then, depending on the weather, wait a few days and feel the soil. Don't water again until it feels dry down to the second knuckle of your finger. (You won't be able to go out to dinner anymore because of your black fingernails, but that is a small sacrifice.) Most geraniums grow best in moderately damp soil, but you can allow them to partially dry out between watering. Geraniums from Mediterranean-type climates are the most drought resistant, as are those with long taproots that can go deep into the soil or grow among the protection of rocks. Water deeply and well, let the plant gradually dry, and then water again.

Multicolored *Geranium pratense* 'Striatum' in full flower at the Ganzel garden in Oregon.

Planting and Ongoing Maintenance

Most geraniums are bought from a nursery or grown from seed and potted up to a size where you can safely plant them outside. Try to plant in spring, after the last frost, even if the geranium is cold tolerant—for the first year of growth it is better to provide a little pampering. Follow the classic recommendation to dig a $100 hole for a $5 plant. The geranium is going to grow better if you amend the planting area with compost, sand or grit, or additives that make the soil slightly acidic, neutral, or slightly alkaline. Learn about your plant before you start. If it is found in nature in an alpine meadow, it is not going to thrive in a shade garden with ferns.

Most geraniums will grow quite rapidly, but a few take several years to build up clump sizes to hold their own in planting schemes. Some of the slow ones, including *Geranium pratense*, *G. psilostemon*, and *G.* 'Rozanne', can become very large when established, as can alpine geraniums like *G. cinereum*. Rapidly growing geraniums include *G.* ×*oxonianum*, *G. phaeum*, *G.* 'Brookside', and *G.* 'Orion'.

Most geraniums flower in spring, although some have quite a long flowering period. Many benefit from a mid-season haircut, particularly those with heavy spring flowering, such as forms of *Geranium* ×*oxonianum*. You can cut the plant to within several inches of the crown and it will rapidly renew the leaves and produce more flowers. Prune back the woody stem geraniums from South Africa to 12 inches (30 cm) after heavy spring flowering. You can shear evergreen ground cover geraniums, such as *G. macrorrhizum* and *G.* ×*cantabrigiense*, with a pair of garden shears, which forces the woody stems to make more growing points. You can also fertilize at this time; new leaves and very often new flowers will grow within about a six-week period. Many geraniums flower on seasonal extending flowering stems, which can get long and look very untidy. You can cut them back to a few inches above the crown. However, cutting back *G. sanguineum* will often mean the end of flowers for the season. Just give it a light haircut to remove the seed heads (unless you want seedlings in your garden). Some gardeners like to deadhead their geraniums after flowering in order to cut back on the number of seedlings.

It is possible to lift and divide hardy geraniums. Wait until the third year, then lift them with a garden fork to cause the least damage to the roots. Dividing with your hands also causes less root damage; use a fork or secateurs as a last resort. After dividing, trim the leaves and replant them in amended soil and water well to settle them in. If you do this in spring after the last frost, the plant should start growing quite rapidly. In mild winter areas, you can divide in fall, as the ground temperatures will encourage growth until the end of November.

You can do a general geranium cleanup at the end of the growing season in mild climates and at the beginning in cold climates. If you cut back some hardy geraniums to a few inches above the crown, new leaves and often new flowers will follow within a month to six weeks. Other geraniums, such as the alpine plants, just need old leaves and flowering stems removed.

Geranium 'Rozanne' has a generous display of flowers from spring to fall.

Pests and Diseases

If you search for information about pests and diseases for geraniums on the web, you will inevitably be directed to the genus *Pelargonium*. The good news is that there is not much advice for the treatment of diseases and pests in the genus Geranium, as these plants are generally carefree. Some bacterial and fungal diseases occur only in particular areas of the United States. If your plant is infected and noninvasive methods fail to ameliorate the problem, consult your county agricultural agent, the United States Department of Agriculture, or the plant pathology department of a local college or university.

SLUGS, SNAILS, RABBITS, AND DEER

Hardy geraniums do not seem to attract slugs and snails, with the exception of the variegated forms of *Geranium phaeum*. However, if slugs and snails are widespread in your garden, try to eradicate them. Although rabbits have been reported to eat hardy geraniums, this does not seem to be a widespread problem. Geraniums appear on lists of plants that are seldom damaged by these creatures. Deer will eat hardy geraniums except the scented-leaf species, *G. macrorrhizum*, and to a lesser extent *G. ×cantabrigiense*. They may or may not eat the flowers of both species, but rarely the leaves. If deer are a problem in your garden, try spreading something that smells disagreeable, such as blood and bone, around newly planted geraniums. This is also a fertilizer, and thus serves a dual purpose, but you must renew it after irrigation or rain. You can also use a commercial product that smells of rotten eggs or something similar. Of course, the most realistic solution is a fence.

BACTERIAL AND FUNGAL LEAF SPOTS

Bacterial leaf spot (*Xanthomonas geranii, Pseudomonas erodii*) develops small, dark spots on the leaves that gradually get larger and coalesce. The spots release bacterial ooze. They are sometimes ringed by yellow, which means that the bacteria are moving into the surrounding leaf tissue. Bacterial leaf spot most commonly develops during hot weather. Fungal leaf spot (there are nine types of fungi, but few appear on cultivated geraniums) has sunken spots on the leaves that gradually get dark and result in patches of dead tissue, or tiny expanding circular spots that will engulf the entire leaf. Fungal leaf spot tends to develop in cool, moist weather.

It is possible to keep leaf spot under control by watering early so the leaves and the top of the soil dry before the end of the day. Use drip or ground-level irrigation whenever possible, and provide good air circulation by spacing the plants so they are not touching. Clean up the plant, leaves, and stems, if necessary, when all are dry, and dispose of them in the garbage, not the compost. Be sure to remove dead plants promptly, disinfect garden tools with denatured alcohol, and wash your hands so you do not transmit the diseases to uninfected plants.

RUST

Rust (*Puccinia leveillei, Puccinia polygoni-amphibii, Uromyces geranii*) is a fungal pathogen that can spread when plants are grown close together. Rust-colored spores appear on the undersides of leaves and can produce discolored, spotty, yellow foliage and some leaf drop. Rust is not a common pathogen for hardy geraniums: it has been seen on *Geranium phaeum*, and on one occasion on *G. ×oxonianum*. This disease is much more common in zonal pelargoniums. To treat, remove the damaged leaves when the plant is dry. You can control rust by maintaining good air circulation, cleaning up all infected leaves, and even cutting down plants and bagging them to put into the trash (not the compost). If a plant is infected, water at ground level rather than with an overhead sprinkler, and do regular cleanup. If the problem persists, it may be necessary to find a geranium species that is more resistant.

POWDERY MILDEW

Powdery mildew (*Erysiphe polygoni*, *Sphaerotheca macularis*) is a fungal disease that causes powdery gray or white patches on the leaves and stems of infected geraniums. If you look through a hand lens, it is possible to see thread-like structures. Powdery mildew generally appears in midsummer. It is particularly bad on *Geranium pratense*, but also infects some selections of *G. sanguineum*. It seldom kills the plants, but they will look unsightly. Try watering plants early in the day so the leaves dry before nightfall. Allowing for good air circulation does help, but it may be necessary to cut the plants back to the ground. Avoid late-summer applications of nitrogen fertilizer, which may exacerbate the problem.

DOWNY MILDEW

This fungal disease, *Plasmopara geranii*, causes unsightly colored patches on the back of leaves and mildew on their upper surfaces. Give plants plenty of space, keep the leaves and stems as dry as possible, and water early in the day so the leaves and soil have time to dry. A location in full sun also helps.

LEAF GALL

Synchytrium geranii, or leaf gall, is a very rare problem, and has not been seen on cultivated hardy geraniums, though it apparently occurs in several wild species, including *Geranium carolinianum*.

Propagation Techniques

Hardy geraniums are usually propagated in one of eight ways, depending on the plant. Willow bark powder, a natural fungicide, aids plant health and good root growth. You can use it to dip the ends of geraniums whose stems have to be cut. When propagating an unknown geranium, dig one up or shake it out of its container and take a look at the structure before you start cutting. Remember to attach a label to any propagated plant that includes the plant name and date it was planted.

CROWN DIVISION

The great majority of geraniums are clump forming. You can divide their crowns, which are usually packed together just above ground. Separate each growing point within the clump by pulling it apart with your hands or separating it with a sharp knife, being careful not to separate your fingers in the process. (Wear gloves!) Your hands will cause less root damage than a knife. Make sure pieces of root are attached, and pot up divisions in the usual way. Geraniums that are good subjects for crown division include *Geranium phaeum*, *G. pratense*, *G. sylvaticum*, and *G. platypetalum*.

Separate
crown with
roots

Cut

▲ Crown division cutting.

▶ Stem cuttings.

Square cut

Make cutting 1½ in. long

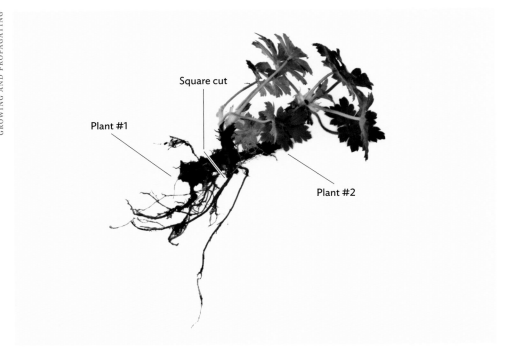

Plant #1

Square cut

Plant #2

◀ Rhizomatous roots.

▼ Flowering stems.

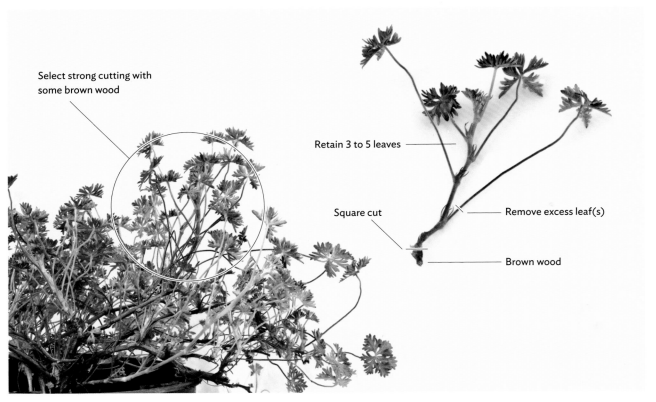

Select strong cutting with
some brown wood

Retain 3 to 5 leaves

Square cut

Remove excess leaf(s)

Brown wood

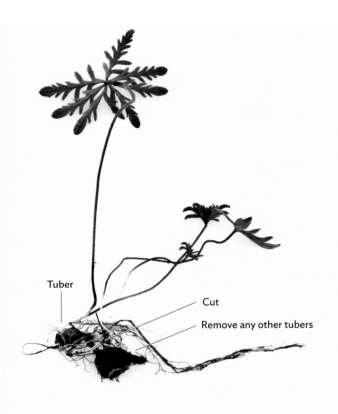

Tuber

Cut

Remove any other tubers

Tubers.

STEM CUTTINGS

Some geraniums, including most alpine species, have a single tap-like root and a caulescent or above-ground crown with growing points with leaves that elongate from it. It is analogous to a view of your forearm, palm, and fingers. You can remove small sections (about 1.5 to 3 inches [3.8–7.5 cm]) of these growing points with a sharp knife or clippers. Pull off dead remains of old leaves and insert the pieces for about half their length into a light, well-drained sterile medium in a small container. Place the containers in a light, bright, but not sunny location until growth recommences. Good geraniums for stem cutting include *Geranium argenteum*, *G. farreri*, and *G.* Cinereum Group. You can use this technique on geraniums that develop subsidiary growing points from a central taproot. These growing points can be separated only by taking a cutting that includes a small piece of the taproot itself, but be careful not to cause major damage to the taproot. If you separate these embryonic plants with a sharp knife and pot them up, they will develop roots. A good example is *G. viscosissimum*.

RHIZOMATOUS ROOTS

You can separate geraniums with growing points on their rhizomatous roots from the parent by pulling the roots apart or cutting sections of the roots with a sharp knife. Pot up pieces with growing points in small containers by laying the roots horizontally and covering with 1 inch (2.5 cm) or so of soil. Put containers in a light, bright, but not sunny place until growth commences. Suitable geraniums include *Geranium ×cantabrigiense*, *G. dalmaticum*, and *G. macrorrhizum*.

WOODY PERENNIAL FLOWERING STEMS

Some geraniums resemble the genus Pelargonium in that you can propagate them from their woody flowering stems. Do not confuse these stems with the annual flowering stems of other geraniums, such as *Geranium pratense*, as the latter will not root. Take 3- to 4-inch (7.5–10 cm) pieces of stem, usually a piece with a growing point, a little green wood, and a small heel of brown wood stem, if possible. Strip off the lower leaves and insert at least two nodes into a light, fast-draining growing medium. Place in a light, bright, but not sunny location until roots are established. You can propagate most of the geraniums from South Africa in this manner, such as *G. harveyi*, *G. incanum*, *G. multisectum*, *G. magniflorum*, and *G. pulchrum*.

TUBERS

There are only a few tuberous rooted geranium species, but they are extremely easy to propagate. These species will go dormant in the summer, and you can lift and separate their tubers and store them in a dry medium, such as sand (it's hard to find them in finely ground bark), in a cool, dry location until planting begins in the fall where the winters are mild. In cold-winter areas, lift tubers in summer, store, and start them in fall in a cool greenhouse or in early spring in the garden. Plant them in a horizontal manner, as it is sometimes difficult to see which end is growing, and cover with several inches of soil. Some tuberous rooted geraniums can tolerate small amounts of water when they are dormant, such as *Geranium libani*, which, if watered, will retain its leaves during the summer. Geraniums whose roots are tuberous include *G. tuberosum*, *G. macrostylum*, *G. malviflorum*, and *G. orientaltibeticum*.

ROOT CUTTINGS

Root cuttings are usually the method of last resort for home gardeners, although this is sometimes the only way to propagate a rare or slow-growing plant. Losses can be high when using this method. Select the thickest possible roots and remove only one or two roots from each plant. Cut roots into 2-inch (5 cm) lengths and plant to maintain their original orientation. (Make a slanted cut for the top section and a square cut for the bottom so you can easily distinguish.) Insert pieces of root into a sterile growing medium with approximately $1/10$ inch (0.3 cm) above the surface. Carefully water and drain the container, and cover the top with a plastic bag held in place with a rubber band. Place in a light, bright, but not sunny location. Heating cables that hold the soil temperature at about 68°F (20°C) are helpful. Check plants frequently to ensure that the soil does not dry out. When growth commences, separate and pot up the individual roots. Plants that lend themselves to root cuttings include *Geranium psilostemon* and its cultivars and hybrids, as well as the double forms of *G. pratense*—'Plenum Caeruleum', 'Plenum Violaceum', and 'Plenum Album'.

SEED

After collecting geranium seed, store it in a cool dry place in a paper (not plastic) bag until ready to sow, usually the following fall or winter. It is very important to label all seed with name, location (if wild collected), and date collected. Continue to record this information after the seed germinates and the small plants are separated.

If the mericarp is still attached to the seed, use needle-nose or wood-splinter tweezers to peel it off. The mericarp can be somewhat rubbery and hairy or dry and brittle. If you are working with a large quantity of seed, a lighted magnifying glass on a stand that leaves the hands free is also helpful. Hold the seed down flat and break off the awn (tail). Fingernails and tweezers are the best tools. Some geranium seed is quite small, and a magnifying glass is essential. All seeds germinate readily if the second seed coat or testa is punctured by a fine pin (the end of the needle-nose tweezers works well). Look for the blunt end of the seed. It needs only a slight prick or scratch; if you exert too much pressure, you can damage the cotyledon of the seed or split the seed in half. Sow the seed immediately in sterilized soil in a small container to the depth of $1/10$ to $1/4$ inch (0.3–0.6 cm), depending on the seed size. Carefully water containers and place in a light, bright, but not sunny location until seed germination occurs, usually within one or two weeks. Seeds will germinate readily at 68° to 70°F (20–21°C), and soil heating cables are useful to produce controlled temperatures. Geraniums that can be propagated from seed include *Geranium maderense*, *G.*

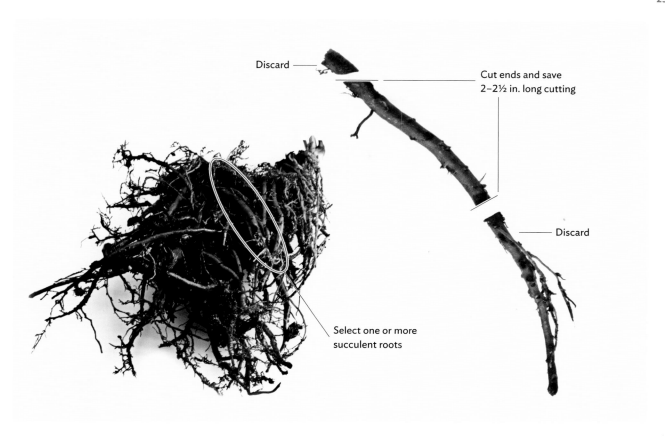

Discard

Cut ends and save
2–2½ in. long cutting

Discard

Select one or more
succulent roots

▲ Root cuttings.

▶ How to prepare seed for
sowing.

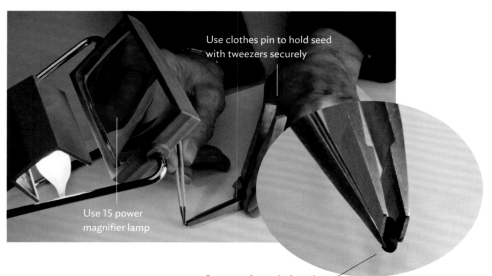

Use clothes pin to hold seed
with tweezers securely

Use 15 power
magnifier lamp

Puncture fat end of seed
with sharp-pointed instrument

palmatum, *G. brutium*, and especially the rare and difficult species, like *G. argenteum*, *G. swatense*, *G. lambertii*, and many others.

TISSUE CULTURE OR MICROPROPAGATION

This is outside the province of the home gardener, but large commercial companies propagate many geraniums by this method. *Geranium* 'Rozanne' is tissue cultured in the Netherlands and produced in South Africa. Geraniums in varying states of growth are shipped all over the world. A number of geraniums are patented and their propagation is restricted to licensed propagators. Check the status of your plant before you propagate it.

Much-beloved *Geranium* 'Johnson's Blue' flowering by a gravel path in Gary Ratway and Deborah Whigham's garden.

WHERE TO BUY

Includes sources for both plants and seeds.

AUSTRALIA

Lambley Nursery
395 Lesters Road
Ascot, Victoria 3364
www.lambley.com.au

AUSTRIA

Sarastro Stauden
Christian H. Kress
4974 Ort im Innkreis 131
www.sarastro-stauden.com

BELGIUM

Algera
Geranium and Perennial Plant Nursery
Hombeek, Antwerpen
www.algera.be

Vaste Planten kwekerij Jo Bogaerts
Frijselstraat 40
1910 Kampenhout
www.vasteplantenjobogaerts.be

GERMANY

Gärtnerei Simon
Staudenweg 2
97828 Marktheidenfeld
www.gaertnerei-simon.de

LATVIA

Rare Bulb Nursery
Dr. Jānis Rukšāns
Vecpulkas
LV-4151 Stalbe
www.rarebulbs.lv
For tuberous rooted geraniums.

NETHERLANDS

Coen Jansen Vaste Planten
Ankummer Es 13a
7722 RD Dalfsen
www.coenjansenvasteplanten.nl

Jan Neelen Vaste Planten
Hemmerbuurt 106
1607 CM Hem
www.janneelenvasteplanten.nl

Kwekerij 'De Hessenhof'
Miranda en Hans Kramer
Hessenweg 41
6718 TC Ede
www.hessenhof.nl

Kwekerij De Kleine Plantage
Handerweg 1
9967 TC Eenrum
www.dekleineplantage.nl

SOUTH AFRICA

Silverhill Seeds
P.O. Box 53108
Kenilworth, 7745 Cape Town
www.silverhillseeds.co.za

UNITED KINGDOM

Beeches Nursery
Crown Hill
Ashdon
Nr. Saffron Walden
Essex CB10 2HB
England
www.beechesnursery.co.uk

Bluebell Cottage Gardens & Nursery
Lodge Lane
Dutton
Near Warrington
Cheshire WA4 4HP
England
www.bluebellcottage.co.uk

Border Alpines
Chasty Court
Chasty Lane
Chasty
Holsworthy
Devon EX22 6NA
England
www.borderalpines.co.uk

Bressingham Gardens
Blooms Nurseries
Bressingham
Diss
Norfolk IP22 2AB
England
www.bressinghamgardens.com

Chadwell Seeds
www.chadwellseeds.co.uk/geranium
Seed of Himalayan Geranium *species collection*

Cranesbill Nursery
Greenhayes
Westmancote
Tewkesbury GL20 7ES
England
www.cranesbillnursery.com

Crûg Farm Plants
Griffith's Crossing
Caernarfon
Gwynedd LL55 1TU
Wales
www.crug-farm.co.uk

Elworthy Cottage Plants
Elworthy
Taunton
Somerset TA4 3PX
England
www.elworthy-cottage.co.uk

The Geraniaceae Group Seed List and Seed Exchange
www.geraniaceae-group.org
Must be a member to participate. For membership, visit the website.

Kilver Court Nursery and Gardens
Ian and Teresa Moss
Kilver Court
Kilver Street
Shepton Mallet
Somerset BA4 5NF
England
www.hardyandunusualplants.co.uk
Postal address only.

The Plantsman's Preference
South Lopham
Norfolk IP22 2LW
England
www.plantpref.co.uk

West Acre Gardens
Tumbleyhill Road
West Acre
King's Lynn
Norfolk PE32 1UJ
England
www.westacregardens.co.uk

Arrowhead Alpines
1310 North Gregory Road
P.O. Box 857
Fowlerville, Michigan 48836
www.arrowheadalpines.com

Cranesbill Nursery
30 New Meadow Road
Swansea, Massachusetts 02777
www.cranesbillnursery.net

Digging Dog Nursery
31101 Middle Ridge Road
Albion, California 95410
www.diggingdog.com

Edelweiss Perennials
29800 S Barlow Road
Canby, Oregon 97013
www.edelweissperennials.com

Geraniaceae Nursery
122 Hillcrest Avenue
Kentfield, California 94904
www.geraniaceae.com

Joy Creek Nursery
20300 Northwest Watson Road
Scappoose, Oregon 97056
www.joycreek.com

Lazy S'S Farm Nursery
2360 Spotswood Trail
Barboursville, Virginia 22923
www.lazyssfarm.com
Online sales only.

Plant Delights Nursery
9241 Sauls Road
Raleigh, North Carolina 27603
www.plantdelights.com

**Sandy's Plants: Rare and Unusual
Perennials**
8011 Bell Creek Road
Mechanicsville, Virginia 23111
www.sandysplants.com

Sunny Border Nurseries
1709 Kensington Road
P.O. Box 483
Kensington, Connecticut 06037
www.sunnyborder.com
For retail sales, click "Find a Retailer."

WHERE TO SEE

The nurseries and collections listed here have varying business hours during different seasons, and some require advance notice if you would like a tour. Be sure to check the websites for visitor information before dropping in.

FRANCE

Dominique Evrard
L'Essentiel sur les Géraniums Vivaces
www.geraniums-vivaces.fr
French National Collection of perennial geraniums.

UNITED KINGDOM

Bressingham Gardens
Blooms Nurseries
Bressingham
Diss
Norfolk IP22 2AB
England
www.bressinghamgardens.com

National Plant Collection of *Geranium* (Species & Primary Hybrids)
Cambridge University Botanic Garden
1 Brookside
Cambridge CB2 1JE
England
www.botanic.cam.ac.uk/Botanic/
Home.aspx

National Collection of *Geranium sylvaticum*
Gary Bartlett
Riddle Road Allotments
Riddle Road
Sittingbourne
Kent ME10 1LF
England
bartlett4@supanet.com

National Collection of *Geranium sylvaticum* and *G. renardii*
Susan Clarke
Wren's Nest
Wrenbury Heath Road
Wrenbury, Nantwich
Cheshire CW5 8EQ
England
wrenburysue@gmail.com

National Collection of *Geranium phaeum* group
Jean Purkiss
1 Kelton Croft
Kirkland, Frizington
Cumbria, CA26 3YE
England
expressplants@aol.com

National Collection of *Geranium ×cantabrigiense, G. macrorrhizum,* and *G. sanguineum*
Margaret Stone
Brockamin
Old Hills
Callow End
Worcestershire WR2 4TQ
England
stone.brockamin@btinternet.com

National Collection of *Geranium nodosum*
Joan Taylor
Silverwood House
Gardeners Lane
Near Romsey
Hampshire SO51 6AD
England
www.birchwoodplants.co.uk

UNITED STATES

Chicago Botanic Garden
1000 Lake Cook Road
Glencoe, Illinois 60022
www.chicagobotanic.org/visit

Digging Dog Nursery
31101 Middle Ridge Road
Albion, California 95410
www.diggingdog.com

Geraniaceae Nursery
122 Hillcrest Avenue
Kentfield, California 94904
www.geraniaceae.com

Joy Creek Nursery
20300 NW Watson Road
Scappoose, Oregon 97056
www.joycreek.com

Niche Gardens
1111 Dawson Road
Chapel Hill, North Carolina 27516
www.nichegardens.com

Northwest Garden Nursery
86813 Central Road NW
Eugene, Oregon 97402
www.northwestgardennursery.com

Plant Delights Nursery
9241 Sauls Road
Raleigh, North Carolina 27603
www.plantdelights.com

FOR MORE INFORMATION

PRINTED MATERIALS

Bath, Trevor, and Joy Jones. 1994. *Hardy Geraniums*. Devon, England: David and Charles.

Bendtsen, Birgitte Husted. 2005. *Gardening with Hardy Geraniums*. Portland, Oregon: Timber Press.

Bendtsen, Birgitte Husted. 2012. *Storkenaeb: Bogen Om Geranium*. Denmark: Narayana Press.

Brenzel, Kathleen Norris, ed. 2012. *The New Sunset Western Garden Book: The Ultimate Gardening Guide*. 9th ed. New York: Time Home Entertainment.

Chase, A. R., Margery Daughtrey, and Gary W. Simone. 1995. *Diseases of Annuals and Perennials: A Ball Guide: Identification and Control*. Batavia, Illinois: Ball Publishing.

The Geraniaceae Group. 1981–2015. *Group News Bulletin*. Various eds. Kent, England: The Geraniaceae Group.

The Geraniaceae Group. 2004. The Geranium Species Checklist: Geranium Knuth Tribe I Geraniaceae. *The Geranium Species Check List Series* 5(1). Comp. R. Clifton. Kent, England: The Geraniaceae Group.

The Geraniaceae Group. 2008. *Register of Geranium Cultivar Names*. 3rd ed. Comp. David Victor. Kent, England: The Geraniaceae Group.

Griswold, Mac, and Eleanor Weller. 1991. *The Golden Age of American Gardens*. New York: Harry N. Abrams.

Hardy Geranium Group. 1998. *Hardy Geranium Group Newsletter*. Autumn. Evesham, England.

Hawke, Richard. 2012. "Geraniums: The Best of the Best." *Fine Gardening* 145 (June): 39–45.

Hibberd, David. 1994. *Hardy Geraniums*. London: the Royal Horticultural Society.

Hilliard, O. M. and B. L. Burtt. 1987. *The Botany of the Southern Natal Drakensberg*. Cape, South Africa: National Botanic Gardens.

Horst, R. Kenneth. 1990. *Westcott's Plant Disease Handbook*. 5th ed. New York: Van Nostrand Reinhold.

Ingwersen, Walter. 1946. *The Genus Geranium*. Pamphlet. London: East Grinstead.

Johnson, A. T. 1927. *A Garden in Wales*. London: Edward Arnold & Company.

Noble, Phoebe. 1994. *My Experience Growing Hardy Geraniums*. Sidney, British Columbia, Canada: Trio Investments.

Pirone, Pascal P. 1978. *Diseases and Pests of Ornamental Plants*. 5th ed. New York: John Wiley & Sons.

Pooley, Elsa. 2003. *Mountain Flowers: A Field Guide to the Flora of the Drakensberg and Lesotho*. Durbin, South Africa: The Flora Publications Trust.

Royal Horticultural Society. 2015. *The RHS Plant Finder*. Lord, Tony. London: Dorling Kindersley.

Rukšāns, Jānis. 2007. *Buried Treasures: Finding and Growing the World's Choicest Bulbs*, Portland, Oregon: Timber Press.

Thompson, Dennis. 1984. "Hardy Geraniums." *Pacific Horticulture* (Fall): 17–21.

Yeo, Peter F. 2002. *Hardy Geraniums*. 2nd ed. Portland, Oregon: Timber Press.

WEBSITES

Al Schneider
Wildflowers, Ferns, and Trees of the Four Corners Region of Colorado, New Mexico, Arizona and Utah.
www.swcoloradowildflowers.com

Flora of the Hawaiian Islands
Smithsonian National Museum of Natural History Collection
Hawaiian Geraniums Image Gallery
botany.si.edu/pacificislandbiodiversity/hawaiianflora/imagegallery.cfm
In the search field titled "Family," enter or scroll to "Geraniaceae," then click "Submit."

The Geraniaceae Group
www.geraniaceae-group.org

Geranium Collection Photo Album
M. van der Veer-de Vries
geraniumfoto.nl
(Dutch)

Geranium Page
Donn Reiners Photography
www.geraniumpage.com

Geranium Taxonomic Information System
Carlos Aedo
www.geranium.es

Hardy Plant Society: Hardy Geranium Group
hardy-plant.org.uk/geranium

Harvard University Herbaria & Libraries
Herbarium Online
www.huh.harvard.edu
Herbaria Geranium Directory: kiki.huh.harvard.edu/databases/specimen_search.php?family=Geraniaceae

Missouri Botanical Garden Plant Finder
www.missouribotanicalgarden.org/plantfinder/plantfindersearch.aspx

National Gardening Association Plant Finder
www.garden.org/plantfinder

Register of *Geranium* Cultivar Names
www.geraniaceae-group.org/geranium_register.02.html

Rein ten Klooster's Geraniums
Groei & Bloei Afdeling Breda
www.breda.groei.nl/index.php?id=29416
(Dutch)

Royal Horticultural Society
www.rhs.org.uk/plants/search-form

Storchschnabel und andere Stauden
Katrin Luger Bauer's Geranium and Garden Homepage
www.geranium.at
(German)

University of Minnesota
What's Wrong With My Plant? Hardy Geraniums
www.extension.umn.edu/garden/diagnose/plant/annualperennial/hardygeranium

HARDINESS ZONE TEMPERATURES

USDA ZONES & CORRESPONDING TEMPERATURES

Temp °F			Zone	Temp °C		
−60	to	−55	1a	−51	to	−48
−55	to	−50	1b	−48	to	−46
−50	to	−45	2a	−46	to	−43
−45	to	−40	2b	−43	to	−40
−40	to	−35	3a	−40	to	−37
−35	to	−30	3b	−37	to	−34
−30	to	−25	4a	−34	to	−32
−25	to	−20	4b	−32	to	−29
−20	to	−15	5a	−29	to	−26
−15	to	−10	5b	−26	to	−23
−10	to	−5	6a	−23	to	−21
−5	to	0	6b	−21	to	−18
0	to	5	7a	−18	to	−15
5	to	10	7b	−15	to	−12
10	to	15	8a	−12	to	−9
15	to	20	8b	−9	to	−7
20	to	25	9a	−7	to	−4
25	to	30	9b	−4	to	−1
30	to	35	10a	−1	to	2
35	to	40	10b	2	to	4
40	to	45	11a	4	to	7
45	to	50	11b	7	to	10
50	to	55	12a	10	to	13
55	to	60	12b	13	to	16
60	to	65	13a	16	to	18
65	to	70	13b	18	to	21

FIND HARDINESS MAPS ON THE INTERNET.
United States usna.usda.gov/Hardzone/ushzmap.html
Canada planthardiness.gc.ca
Europe houzz.com/europeZoneFinder

ACKNOWLEDGMENTS

This book is dedicated to Sinclaire McCredie Parer, formerly PIP, when she made her first appearance in print. She loves flowers and cares about the environment, and that is a good beginning.

Very grateful thanks for Tom Fischer for his kindly persistence in encouraging me to write, to Linda Willms and Sarah Rutledge Gorman for help with the manuscript, and to Sarah Milhollin for overseeing and selecting photographs.

A huge thank you to Donn Reiners for fine photographs of the geraniums taken over a number of years. He has been so generous with his time and has shown great skill and patience, particularly in getting those troublesome blue and pink flower colors, so prevalent in geraniums, just right. Thank you to Saxon Holt for his elegant and lyrical photos and to Rachel Etheridge for her photographic contributions and for so generously sharing her vast knowledge of the genus *Geranium*.

Special thanks to Tim Fuller of The Plantman's Preference and to Kevin Marsh of Beeches Nursery, who allowed me to take up much busy time and pore over their large collection of hardy geraniums over several visits to the United Kingdom. Thank you to Bleddyn and Sue Wynn-Jones of Crûg Farm Plants, Wales, for showing me such generosity and hospitality, as well as the freedom to wander among their extensive collection of hardy geraniums. I hold them partially responsible for my unseemly interest in these addictive plants.

And, finally, thanks to two very special people: James Kleier, Jr., for organizing me and for cheerful and unstinting help with the manuscript, fact-checking, and keeping us on an even keel; and my husband, Bill Parer, for his total support, always.

PHOTO CREDITS

Photos by Donn Reiners, except as noted below.

RACHEL ETHERIDGE, pages 52 top, 59, 60 right, 121, 125, 130, 134, 147 right, 157, 164 left, 184, 200 right, 202, 213 left, and 221.

SAXON HOLT, pages 2–3, 10–11, 23, 30–31, 40–41, 42–43, 45, 46, 51 left, 66, 67 top, 68 bottom, 69 left and right, 70, 73, 75 top and botttom, 79 bottom, 82 top right, 88–89, 96 bottom, 97 middle, 100 top, 107, 112 top, 114, 117, 123, 127, 129, 131, 136, 140–141, 144 left, 145 left, 149 left bottom, 151 left, 160 right, 162, 165 left, 166–167, 176 top, 178, 179, 182 bottom, 188, 191 bottom, 195 bottom, 204, 207 left and right, 210 left, 211, 218 right, 222–223, 224–225, 226, 230, 238–239, and 258.

GAP/CHRISTIAN BOLLEN, page 198 right.

GAP/FHF GREENMEDIA, page 132.

GAP/MARCUS HARPUR, page 203 top.

GAP/SUE HEATH, front cover.

GAP/HOWARD RICE, page 124.

SHUTTERSTOCK/BILDAGENTUR ZOONAR GMBH, page 113.

SHUTTERSTOCK/HIPPRODUCTIONS, page 215 right.

WIKIMEDIA/DOMINICUS JOHANNES BERGSMA, page 206—used under a Creative Commons Attribution–Share Alike 3.0 Unported License.

WIKIMEDIA/Σ64, page 133—used under a GFDL and Creative Commons Attribution–Share Alike 3.0 Unported License.

INDEX

ABOUT THE AUTHOR

ROBIN PARER is the owner of Geraniaceae, a mail-order nursery in Marin County, California, specializing in members of the geranium family, including 398 varieties of hardy geranium. She is a co-organizer of the Bay Area Horticultural Society (the "Hortisexuals") and a frequent lecturer, renowned both for the depth of her knowledge and her disarming humor. Visit her at geraniaceae.com.

SAXON HOLT

Front cover: *Geranium* 'Ann Folkard'
Spine: *Geranium renardii* (top), *G. cataractarum* (bottom)
Title page: *Geranium* 'Ann Folkard'
Contents page: *Geranium pratense* 'Striatum'

Published in 2016 by Timber Press, Inc.

The Haseltine Building
133 S.W. Second Avenue, Suite 450
Portland, Oregon 97204-3527
timberpress.com

Library of Congress Cataloging-in-Publication Data
Parer, Robin, author.
    The plant lover's guide to hardy geraniums/Robin Parer.—First
    edition.
       pages cm
    Includes index.
    ISBN 978-1-60469-418-5
    1. Hardy geraniums. 2. Geraniums. I. Title. II. Title: Hardy
    geraniums.
    SB413.G35P37 2016
    635.9'3379—dc23   2015029659

A catalog record for this book is also available from the British
Library.

Series design by Laken Wright
Cover design by Kristi Pfeffer
Printed in China

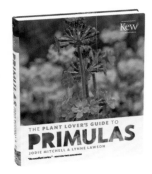

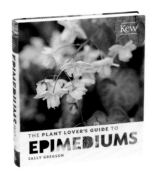